How to Finish Your PhD

by Catherine Pope

2020

ISBN 978-1-8382429-0-9

Contents

Introduction   5

1. What's the Purpose of a PhD?   14

2. Getting Ready to Do Things Differently   29

3. Making a Plan   46

4. Working with Your Supervisor   67

5. Managing Competing Priorities   97

6. Becoming a More Productive Writer   125

7. Building Routines and Keeping Going   163

8. Getting Ready for Submission   186

Conclusion   227

Bibliography   231

Acknowledgements   233

Index   235

Introduction

"The one thing more difficult than following a
regimen is not imposing it in others." - Marcel
Proust

Just after I finished my PhD, I had lunch with a friend I'd
not seen for a little while. When she asked what I'd been
up to, it was very satisfying to produce a photo of myself in my doctoral plumage. "Blimey, Catherine," she said,
"you must've worked *really* hard". "Yes," I replied, smiling broadly and triumphantly. The smile faded as she added, "because it's not as though you're really intelligent or
anything".

Within this most backhanded of compliments lurks an
essential truth: successfully completing your PhD is down
to diligence, not brilliance. Of course, you need a good idea
to start with and the insight to turn it into a significant and
original research project; but then it's a case of organising
and motivating yourself. That's what this book is all about.

Over the last six years, I've worked with more than
3,000 students at different stages of their PhD. Although

many were struggling, not one lacked the intellectual capabilities to produce a thesis. The problem was always confidence, time management, or lack of direction — sometimes all three. I'm here to help you get back on track and reach the finish line.

My Background

I was awarded my PhD by the University of Sussex back in 2014. My subject was the Victorian author Florence Marryat, who wrote dozens of lurid novels and enjoyed a very colourful personal life. I studied part-time, alongside full-time employment, and finished in just under 4 years. This is not because I'm bionic – far from it – but because I treated my PhD like a project. That's to say that I broke everything down, set targets, and monitored my progress. Alas, I cannot claim that it always went smoothly. There was a lot of despondency, periods of complete inactivity, and afternoons of shouting at my computer when it was misbehaving. I'll share some of these unedifying episodes with you later on.

Like many researchers, I struggled with feelings of inadequacy, or 'Imposter Syndrome' as it's often called. We'll discuss this in Chapter Two. Finishing my thesis proved more of a psychological than an intellectual challenge. Not recognising this initially, I pushed myself too hard and made the project much more difficult than it needed to be. Now that I'm brimming with post-doctoral wisdom, I hope to prevent you from making some of the same mistakes. Doing a PhD shouldn't be an exercise in masochism. Taking care of your health and wellbeing makes it more likely that you'll succeed. After all, you want to be well enough to enjoy swishing about in your finery on graduation day.

Why I'm Writing this Book

Since graduating, I've spent many hours pondering easier ways of finishing a PhD. After a brief stint as a lecturer, I realised that I love supporting researchers. I've been running workshops, facilitating writing retreats, and offering 1-2-1 coaching at more than a dozen universities. This privileged position has given me an insight into the lives of PhD students from a range of backgrounds and disciplines.

Although everyone is completely different, you're all facing broadly the same challenge: doing a PhD is hard. This becomes even harder if you're combining it with a job or caring responsibilities, or if you're writing in a second language. Given a PhD usually takes between 3 and 6 years, there's a good chance that life will intervene at least once to throw you off course, too. The tired old advice of "Treat your PhD like a job" simply doesn't work. I'm here to offer a more practical perspective.

A few people breeze through their PhD, knowing exactly what they're doing and never giving their supervisor a moment's worry. This probably isn't you. I don't want to present doctoral research as an unbearable slog, but I *do* want to be realistic. It's tough for most of us. That's why relatively few people get to call themselves Dr. It's hard, but not impossible. I want to help make it *possible for you*. My role is to break down each stage so it's more manageable. This book is intended as a pocket coach, providing support when you need it.

Who This Book is For

I'm assuming you're reading this book because you're struggling. This book is mainly aimed at PhD students who have already started on their thesis and have made some progress. You might have entered your second year and suddenly realised that the submission date is closer than you thought. Or you could be in the final stages, trying frantically to bring everything together.

As such, I shan't be addressing the literature review, fieldwork, or data analysis. I'm assuming you've done this already and are now writing up your results. Nor will I dispense advice on developing a theoretical framework or choosing a methodology. If you're still planning your project, there's lots of great advice out there. You can find some reading recommendations in the Bibliography. You might still find a lot of the book helpful, though.

This isn't another "this worked for me, so it'll work for you" book. There's no miracle cure lurking in these pages, just lots of proven strategies for you to try. Some of them are based on my experience, others are from students I've coached over the last six years. Annoyingly, we can't just deploy someone else's successful regimen — it's a matter of trial and error, rather like research itself. I'll offer a range of tools or methods so you can discover what's right for *you*.

There are parts of the book that will resonate with you; other advice might not make any sense at all for your specific situation. Please disregard anything that's not helpful. We're all unique, so no single solution benefits everyone. And please be kind to yourself along the way. I'm not setting standards for you to achieve. It's about creating a sense of curiosity and a willingness to experiment, rather than pursuing perfectionism.

I've tried to make my advice applicable to all disciplines and styles of thesis. Inevitably, though, there are many differences, and you'll need to adapt some of the examples to suit your circumstances. Nevertheless, whether you're based in the laboratory or in the archives, you still need to produce a very long document that makes a contribution to the sum of human knowledge.

Although I'm here to help you complete your thesis, there's only so much I can do. In this book, I'm focusing on the *fundamentals*, the processes that you need to create, deploy, and refine. The next layer is the conventions in *your discipline*. This is where you'll need to talk to your supervisors and peers to find out how this information applies in your particular context. It will vary enormously according to the type of research you're pursuing. And then finally, the very top layer is the specifics for *your project*. Your thesis is completely unique. This means you'll have to adapt what you've learned from me and other people to come up with a solution that's right for you. Nobody else can tell you precisely what you should do with your thesis.

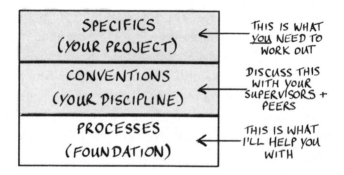

A Note on Language and Terminology

Throughout this book, I'll be referring to your *thesis* — the term generally used in the UK for the written element of the PhD. In the US, it's usually known as the *dissertation*. The Americans are right on this one. The argument based on your research is the *thesis*, and the *dissertation* is the written document in which you explain it. Given I'm based in the UK, I'm going with *thesis*.

There are many different ways of referring to *you*: PhD student, doctoral researcher, postgraduate researcher, and many more. I'm sticking with PhD student. Although some people are keen to emphasise their transition from taught student to researcher, others have told me that being referred to as a *student* is a relief. *Student* suggests they're not yet experts — and that's exactly how they feel. I'm also using this term in the interests of clarity. I'll also refer to PhD *supervisors*. In the US, they're usually known as a dissertation or doctoral advisor.

I use British spelling because anything else just feels odd. And most of my examples and terminology refer exclusively to the UK Higher Education system. While the advice here might be more broadly applicable, you should always consult the regulations for your institution.

How to Use this Book

You can either read this book from cover to cover or simply jump into the chapter that's most relevant for you. I've kept it concise to ensure you don't have to waste time that could be spent on your thesis. Each chapter concludes with a summary of what we've covered, along with some action points and a troubleshooting guide.

This book is arranged in eight chapters, each focused on a specific area of finishing your PhD:

Chapter 1 is all about purpose — understanding exactly what's required from a thesis, and *why* you want to write one. Yes, this *did* seem a good idea at some point. Once you have a sense of purpose, everything else becomes much easier.

In **Chapter 2**, I help you develop the right mindset for finishing your PhD. This includes vanquishing the dreaded Imposter Syndrome and experimenting with some positive psychology. Often, we get stuck in the past, thinking about all the things we *should* have done, rather than focusing on what we can do *now*.

You'll start planning in **Chapter 3**, by setting milestones, anticipating problems, and being realistic. I'll explain that you are the project manager of your PhD and we'll consider what skills and resources you'll need for completion.

An effective working relationship with your supervisor is crucial to your PhD success. In **Chapter 4**, we'll think about how you can get the support you need and also identify potential sources of conflict.

Chapter 5 is dedicated to prioritisation — the business of making sure you do your most important work each day by protecting your time and eliminating distracting thoughts. We can easily get overwhelmed by all the stuff that's beyond our control, while all those priorities slip away.

It's not just about protecting time, we also need to use it effectively. In **Chapter 6**, we'll develop some tactics so you can make significant progress with your writing. By understanding the obstacles that get in our way, we can overcome procrastination and become more focused.

Most of us can achieve a couple of productive days. The challenge is to do this consistently. In **Chapter 7**, we'll create some routines to help you achieve the results you crave. You'll also meet a monkey and discover what you can do on those days when your brain refuses to cooperate.

Finally, in **Chapter 8**, I'll guide you through improving the structure, content, and flow of your thesis. This is the stage where you're thinking about how you *present* your research project to examiners. I'm here to ensure you show it off to the best possible advantage.

Occasionally, I'll recommend technology. As that's an excellent way of rendering a book obsolete in a matter of weeks, I'll be including all the links on my website rather than within the text: www.howtofinishyourphd.com.

Are you ready? Let's get started.

1. What's the Purpose of a PhD?

"If you're not sure why you're doing something, you can never do enough of it." David Allen, *Getting Things Done*

What's the purpose of a PhD? Well, this is a big question. There are two main elements here: the purpose of your *thesis* and *your* purpose in pursuing a PhD. In this chapter, we'll examine both. A sense of purpose is vital to keep you motivated, especially when it gets tough. We've all experienced the Dark Night of the Soul. Everything is terrible, and we have no idea why this project ever seemed like a good idea.

We also need to understand what we're required to do. Often, we plough on without really understanding the objective of a thesis. Stopping to consider the requirements can help us set limits and make this project more manageable. Has your supervisor explained what a thesis is? Probably not. They've no doubt seen dozens if not hundreds of theses during their careers and have forgotten what it's like to be in your position. Maybe you've never even looked at one. It's hard to create something if you're not entirely sure what it looks like.

In this chapter, I'll help you clarify or regain your sense of purpose. Maybe this got lost after the initial excitement faded. By flirting with some neuroscience, I explain why we need to be emotional before we can get rational. Then we'll consider the purpose of the PhD. What exactly is meant by originality and significance? Finally, we'll investigate the limits of PhD so you can contain your project and finish on time.

Why Are You Doing a PhD?

> "To see what is in front of one's nose needs a constant struggle." George Orwell, 'In Front of Your Nose'

Think back. There must've been a point when you were excited about your research. You were a bundle of potential energy, desperate to immerse yourself in this project. That enthusiasm is quickly forgotten when experiencing setbacks, conflicts, and unexpected outcomes.

Firstly, I'd like you to note down your responses to three questions. I know it's annoying when authors insist you do stuff when you're trying to read, so I'll include a reminder at the end of the chapter, too:

» Why do you want to finish your PhD?

» What areas of your research excite or inspire you?

» Why is this project important to you?

When you're struggling with your writing and lots of other responsibilities, it's easy to lose sight of why this ever seemed like a good idea. Written evidence can help. While it can take seconds for our mood to plummet when faced with a problem, we can bounce back just as quickly when confronted with some positive reinforcement.

Also take some time to reflect on why you're doing a PhD. I did this during a particularly dark period, and it was both illuminating and motivating. Illuminating because I realised that most of the reasons were quite shallow. I wanted to call myself 'Dr Pope' and also finish before my partner, who was also a part-time PhD student. Ultimately, though, I concluded that getting this pesky project finished would allow me to move on to other challenges and seize new opportunities.

Here's the list I created:

Reasons to finish my PhD, by Catherine Pope (aged 39 and a half)

1. Call myself Dr

2. Finish before my partner

3. Ensure my idea remains original

4. Sense of achievement

5. New opportunities

6. More time to pursue other projects

7. To prove I can do it

8. Get it done before I turn 40

I missed the final aim by two months, but that was OK. It provided a clear target. I probably could've hit it, but made a conscious decision to slow down in the interests of my health. More of that in Chapter 5.

Give it a try and see what you come up with. I can't see what you write, so don't worry if some of your reasons are similarly shallow. They might seem shallow to other people but remain important to you. There's a worksheet you can download at www.howtofinishyourphd.com.

Refer back to this list if you're struggling. When times are hard, it's easy to convince ourselves that the project is pointless. A quick look at your reasons will remind you why this is important. Keep it pinned to your wall or somewhere else that's easily visible.

Why? is a key question we'll return to throughout this book. In his hugely popular book *Start with Why*, Simon

Sinek explains that when beginning a project, we usually start with the *what* and the *how*. We get bogged down by the mechanics and details, seldom pausing to consider our motivation. It's our neocortex — the rational part of our brain — that deals with *what* and *how*. Although this more evolved area is vital for writing a thesis, it's slow to fire up. The more dominant part of our brain is the limbic area which governs the emotions — this is the bit that's activated very quickly on social media. If we satisfy the emotional reasons for doing something *first*, it's easier to work out exactly *what* we're going to do and *how*.

Later, I'll explain the importance of starting with *why* in your writing, too.

What is a PhD?

One of the reasons why finishing a PhD is so hard is that there's minimal discussion as to what's expected. Of course, the term 'an original and significant contribution to knowledge' is often bandied about, but what does that actually mean? Consequently, our imagination runs riot, and we decide that a doctoral thesis is a Theory of Everything.

My favourite article on writing a thesis is 'It's a PhD, not a Nobel Prize', not least because you need only read the title to get the gist. We often make life difficult for ourselves by setting impossibly high standards, then get frustrated when we can't meet them. The authors explain that the PhD is an *examination*, a point I'll be emphasising throughout this book. They write:

A PhD is a stepping stone into a research career. All you need to do is to demonstrate your capacity for independent, critical thinking. That's all you need to do. A PhD is three years of solid work, not a Nobel Prize.[1]

It might be more than three years of solid work for you, but you get the point. A PhD should be the beginning of your research career, not its culmination. Your magnum opus comes later.

Taking the time to understand exactly what's required makes the project more manageable. You're not trying to win a prize, rather to convince a couple of experts — your examiners — that your research meets the required standard. The main criteria on which a doctoral thesis is judged are *originality* and *significance*. It's got to be something new, but also of importance. Novelty alone is insufficient.

Let's look at those in more detail.

Originality

If you've emerged from a taught programme like a Masters, you're probably used to synthesising existing knowledge and then adding your perspective. At PhD level, you're actually *creating* new knowledge that other people will interpret, discuss, and challenge. You're part of the debate rather than just a spectator. The literal meaning of *thesis* is an original argument. Your examiners want to make sure your project is a

....
1 Mullins, Gerry, and Margaret Kiley, '"It's a PhD, Not a Nobel Prize": How Experienced Examiners Assess Research Theses', *Studies in Higher Education*, 27.4 (2002), 369–86.

thesis and not just a synthesis. You use your literature review to establish a gap or limitation, then you address that gap or limitation with your own original research.

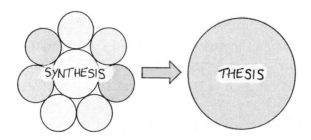

Originality is a common concern that pops up during my workshops and coaching sessions. Students are often anxious that there's nothing new about their research and that they'll fail their viva. The primary cause of this anxiety is, I think, that everyone else's research is now much more visible. We have access to millions of papers, blog posts, and theses online, many of which touch upon our own area.

Twenty years ago, you'd have been only dimly aware of what was happening unless you actively sought those resources in a physical library. Now you glance briefly at a title or abstract online and convince yourself this is *exactly the same* as our thesis. Someone else is working on this topic, so your own efforts are futile or superfluous.

Even if you're working on the same topic as someone else, your approach is likely to be completely different. You probably have a different methodology, dataset, or theoretical framework. As a professional researcher (yes, that's what you are), you bring a *unique* perspective to this research problem.

Significance

Some students grow despondent because they can no longer see the significance of their research. This is especially common in Arts & Humanities subjects. I vividly remember attending a workshop where most of the other students were scientists working on a cure for Alzheimer's. My project seemed frivolous and self-indulgent. In the context of challenges facing the planet, new ideas about an obscure Victorian novelist weren't going to make a jot of difference; in the context of my field, though, I was making a significant contribution. My research addressed an overlooked topic that challenged several misconceptions. We can't all change the world. Don't compare yourself to anyone else, especially if they're beyond your discipline.

We sometimes get carried away with the idea of significance, imagining that our ideas have to be earth-shattering. They seldom are. While your idea needs to be important, that doesn't mean devising a new way to measure gravity. We all make a *tiny* contribution that adds to the sum of human knowledge. You might think of it as crowdsourcing. To use a Wikipedia analogy, you're contributing an article, not trying to write an encyclopedia. And other people will build on your contribution, maybe even challenging it. That's OK. You're part of an ongoing debate rather than having the final word.

The critical point that I want you to keep in mind is that the PhD is an examination with specific requirements that you need to follow. As we've seen, the two main requirements are originality and significance. In Chapter 8, I'll help you make this original and significant contribution visible to your examiners. For now, we need to investigate a few other requirements for a PhD.

Containing Your PhD

When I'm coaching early-stage PhD students, I encourage them to consider the limits of a thesis. We often imagine it as an undefinable and magical beast that emerges at an unspecified point during our programme. No. A thesis is simply a very long document that you submit for examination. Its purpose is to prove to two or three examiners that you have conducted some original research and can defend the arguments that you've made.

A thesis doesn't have to be elegant or exhaustive – it needs to be a clearly structured and well-argued piece of writing that focuses on a particular topic. When students say to me, "But Catherine, you don't understand — my thesis is going to be much more than that," I know they'll never finish. You can pursue all sorts of exciting projects after your PhD – books, radio shows, TV series — the thesis is just your means to get there.

Very few people will read your thesis. Sorry. That's not to say it isn't important, rather that they'll be interested in the outputs *based* on your doctoral research, such as journal articles and monographs. Passing your viva gives you the endorsement necessary to be accepted as an expert in your field. So, just do enough to get your PhD. After all, you don't have time to do any more than that. Understand the requirements of the doctoral thesis for your discipline and institution, then work out exactly what you need to do. And no more. There's no grading system for PhDs. Your examiners won't give you a tiara for doing additional work.

How do I set some limits?

Hopefully, you have a handbook for doctoral researchers, or something similar for your institution. This will specify the word limit, layout, and any special requirements for practice-based PhDs. It can vary enormously according to your subject area, so please scrutinise everything carefully. If anything is unclear, speak to somebody. You might need to amass a variety of guidelines that apply at university, school, and department level.

The most important fact you're seeking is the word limit. This can range from 30,000-100,000 words, so it's crucial to find out what's required. I made the mistake of asking my supervisor, who breezily responded: "Oh, it's 100,000 words, not including the bibliography." I diligently produced a draft that totalled 120,000 words, only to discover the terrible truth. The limit was actually 80,000 words, *including* my bibliography. This meant ditching large chunks of writing.

Never ask your supervisor about regulations. They often feel the need to appear omniscient, so won't necessarily admit to not knowing the answer to a question. Also, they might've overlooked an update to the university's regulations and requirements. Always check the latest version of the handbook, too. You probably also have a research examinations office who can clarify any details for you.

Once you're clear on the number of words, that'll help contain your project. Consider all the apparatus you need to include, for example, the methodology, literature review, and critical framework, and that probably doesn't actually leave much space. Think about how that word count is distributed across your chapters. What will be the weightings? Are you going to break down each chapter into sections? How many words will those sections comprise? You might find that an intimidating section you've been postponing only needs to be 500 words long. Suddenly it's more manageable. Don't do any unnecessary work, as you don't have time. In Chapter 3, we'll work out how you're going to get everything done.

I've seen many theses suffer from 'scope creep', where the student finds an exciting new idea they're desperate to include. Don't be tempted to squeeze it in. A digression will make your thesis baggier and potentially confusing for your examiners. Also, those ideas provide content for future projects. If you want to publish your thesis as a monograph, the publisher will almost certainly request some original material. This is the perfect use for those extra bits and bobs.

. . . .
ACTIVITY
. . . .

Look at your university regulations and find out:

» What are the requirements for your thesis? Word limit? Format?

» When do you need to submit it? Being clear on the date can help focus the mind and avoid overambition. If you're funded, when does the money run out?

» How will your thesis/project be assessed? What are the examiners looking for? See whether there's any specific guidance at your institution.

Conclusion

Identifying your motivation and establishing exactly what's required can give you a jump start on your thesis. All too often, we push ahead blindly without taking the time to work out what we're doing and why. Have you regained your PhD mojo? If not, take a look at the Troubleshooting section at the end.

....
ACTION POINTS
....

1. Remind yourself of your motivation with the following prompts:

> » Why do you want to finish your PhD?

> » What areas of your research excite you or inspire you?

> » Why is this project important to you?

2. Write a list of reasons why you want to finish your PhD.

3. Check the word limit (and any other requirements) for your thesis.

....
SUMMARY
....

> » Start with *why* to remind yourself of the reasons for finishing your PhD. Once you're motivated, it's much easier to work out the *how* and the *what*.

> » The PhD is an examination with specific requirements. Make sure you understand them thoroughly. You don't have time to do more than is necessary.

> » Set some limits on your project to make it more manageable. It's a thesis, not a book or a Nobel Prize.

» Now we've got a sense of purpose, we can prepare to do things differently.

....

TROUBLESHOOTING

....

I'm completely lacking in motivation

If you've tried the exercises and still haven't found your PhD mojo, it's time to think seriously about your next steps. Maybe you have some other big stuff going on in your life, or circumstances have changed, so your PhD is no longer a meaningful goal. Talk to someone at your university to get impartial advice. Most institutions offer confidential counselling for PhD students. This is preferable to talking to your supervisor, who might have a vested interest in your continuing. It's crucial to reach a decision that's right for *you*.

I'm concerned my thesis isn't original or significant

This is a common concern. In this situation, your literature review is there to help. This is the place where you establish the gap you're addressing with your thesis and *why* this gap *needs* to be addressed. Often, the originality and significance are hiding underneath many layers of secondary sources, context, and digressions. In Chapter 8, I'll show you how to peel away those layers to reveal your originality and allow the argument to shine through. I should also add that for many of us, a strong sense of that argument doesn't emerge until embarrassingly late in the PhD process. We just have to keep going and trust that it'll gradually become clear. It will.

I'm getting conflicting information on the requirements for my thesis

Speak to the department responsible for research degrees. They might be called the Graduate School Office, the Research Student Administration Office, or something like that. They're usually responsible for producing the regulations and can give you clear advice. Always listen to them in preference to supervisors, friends, or colleagues — the rules might have changed since they submitted.

2. Getting Ready to Do Things Differently

"Truth is the only safe ground to stand on."
Elizabeth Cady Stanton

Finishing your PhD will be a challenge. As with all challenges, it's much easier if you're mentally prepared and have established the right mindset. This involves achieving a tricky balance between accepting that this is tough, but also believing you can do it. There will be times when your self-doubt is crippling, but other moments where you're in a blissful state of flow.

In this chapter, I'll share some techniques from the world of positive psychology to help you practice self-compassion. You might already be thinking, "No, Catherine, I must be tough on myself, else this thesis will never get done." If so, I'd ask you to reflect on whether that approach has helped

THE PROGRESS OF A THESIS CHAPTER

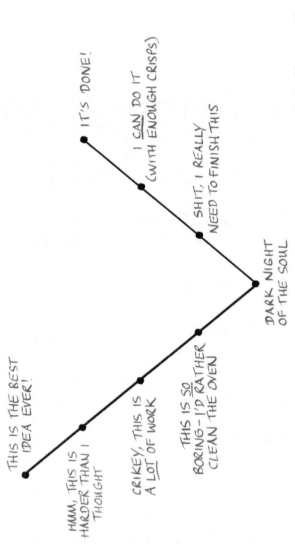

THIS IS THE BEST
IDEA EVER!

HMM, THIS IS
HARDER THAN I
THOUGHT

CRIKEY, THIS IS
A LOT OF WORK

THIS IS SO
BORING – I'D RATHER
CLEAN THE OVEN

DARK NIGHT
OF THE SOUL

SHIT, I REALLY
NEED TO FINISH THIS

I CAN DO IT
(WITH ENOUGH CRISPS)

IT'S DONE!

inspired by Austin Kleon

you so far. Even if you *have* made progress by being a tyrant to yourself, this behaviour won't necessarily serve you during the later stages of your PhD when you're lacking in energy and enthusiasm.

Now we're going to experiment with new ways of thinking. You'll find out how to establish a growth mindset, overcome the dreaded imposter syndrome, and defeat your inner critic. With a few additions to your toolkit, you'll be in a stronger position to cope with anything that arises during your PhD. And maybe beyond, too.

The Progress of a PhD

When things are bad, we can't imagine ever feeling in control; when everything's going well, we imagine we've finally cracked it, and it'll be easy from here. Neither situation is true. The reality is that we're continually pinging between states of euphoria and despair.

On the opposite page, I created a diagram to illustrate our fluctuating emotions throughout a thesis chapter.

We start out brimming with enthusiasm and energy, mercifully oblivious to the trouble ahead. Despondency descends as we realise the drudgery that follows the moments of insight and discovery. At times it can feel overwhelming and impossible — "Why did I ever start a PhD?". Then the wallowing turns to panic — "My funding's running out!" We refocus, lower our standards, and get pedalling. Finally, miraculously, it's done.

The finished thesis isn't quite the Theory of Everything we'd envisaged, but it's *done*. Phew. It doesn't matter how you got there, you're judged only on the final document and your performance in the viva. The examiners won't know about all the wailing and the Pringles. So, accept this is going to be tough.

We'd all like to appear elegant and dignified, but that won't get you extra points. Maybe other researchers seem to be gliding effortlessly through their PhD, but you don't have a backstage pass to their Dark Night of the Soul. And you can be sure that people who share their enviable word counts on social media are overcompensating for other character flaws.

Forgetting the Past

As I mentioned earlier, this book is intended as a pocket coach to support you through your PhD. Unlike counselling, coaching is always focused on the future, rather than picking over what's happened in the past. Whatever's happened in the past stays there — you can't change it. You need all your energy for what comes next. That's the part you *can* control. Of course, you can't control the future directly, but you can decide what you do each day, and this determines what happens next. Those daily actions build up to results. In Chapter 5, we'll spend more time thinking about what's within your control.

To the casual observer, my PhD performance was stellar. Although I was also doing paid work throughout, I finished more quickly than many full-time students. However, there were long periods where absolutely nothing happened. I effectively pretended the PhD didn't exist. Even thinking about it made me feel stressed and tearful. I saw myself as someone who simply wasn't good enough, and this self-image prevented me from making any progress.

In the first year, my plan was straightforward. I had an extensive list of primary sources to interrogate and a well-defined early chapter to draft. Once I moved into the second year, however, things became tougher. I needed to make sense of my research material and decide how to organise it. There were unexpected results that threw me off course, and I was tired. I started ignoring my thesis and thinking I'd come back to it when I was feeling more robust. Time dragged on. At one stage, I completely ignored my thesis for the best part of six months.

This dip is illustrated below in what I call my Incompetence Sandwich:

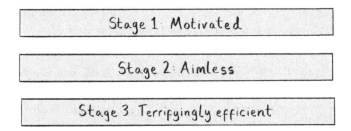

I finally realised that the approach I used in the first year wasn't suitable for the mid-late stages of my PhD. And beating myself up wouldn't help, either. I took the time to rethink my strategy and consider how I could do things differently. After two horrible years, I got around 65% of my thesis done in that final year. I'd worked out my motivation, drawn up a realistic plan, and developed an effective process. Most importantly, I focused on what was coming next. There was absolutely nothing I could do about that filling in my Incompetence Sandwich. Instead, I told myself I was capable of finishing. I developed a *growth mindset*.

Developing a Growth Mindset

Professor Carol Dweck's extensive research has shown that how we think of ourselves profoundly affects the way we lead our lives. Our *mindset* is the view we have of our qualities and characteristics, and whether they can be changed. If you have a *fixed mindset*, you believe that characteristics such as intelligence, personality, and creativity are set: "This is just how I am - there's nothing I can do about it." A *growth mindset*, however, is based on the belief that these qualities can be developed through effort and perseverance.

People with a fixed mindset struggle with setbacks. Problems or unexpected results are evidence of their inadequacy: "See? I told you I'm too stupid to do a PhD." Someone with a growth mindset still experiences those setbacks, but they're likely to view them as an opportunity to learn and develop. They'll also be more receptive to constructive feedback. Rather than attacks, those comments and suggestions are seen as useful input to improve their work. Dweck explains in *Mindset*:

As you become a more growth-minded person, you're amazed at how people start to help you, support you. They no longer seem like adversaries out to deny you what you deserve. They're more and more often collaborators toward a common goal.

....
ACTIVITY
....

What are you struggling with at the moment? What are you telling yourself? If you're saying "I can't do this," try replacing it with "I can't do this *yet*." How does that feel?

Around 5 years ago, a part-time PhD student complained to me that she simply wasn't clever enough to write a thesis. She kept hitting blocks and getting things wrong. "I'm not intelligent, not in that way," she told me. I asked her if she knew anyone who had a PhD. "Oh yes," she replied, "lots, I work in a business school." "How many," I inquired, "do you think are highly intelligent?" Her brow furrowed. There was a long silence, before she finally concluded, "Hmm, there must be something else to it." Those colleagues weren't adult-onset prodigies. They believed in themselves enough to get to the finish line. It's not about arrogance or bloody-mindedness, rather a commitment to keeping going.

A PhD is a big experiment. Even if you're not a scientist, you are still testing out theories, responding to unexpected results, and trying a different approach. We're never going to get it right first time. By learning from our mistakes, we hone our research skills and build resilience. If we flounder at the first obstacle, there's no scope for development. When we're lacking in confidence, we seek evidence to prove our lack of ability, rather than new possibilities — we adopt a fixed mindset, rather than a *growth* mindset. This is when Imposter Syndrome takes hold.

Understanding Imposter Syndrome

Imposter Syndrome,[2] or overwhelming feelings of inadequacy, is well documented and seems to affect most doctoral researchers at least some of the time. What's discussed less often is the fact that it never goes away — it's just less acceptable for tenured academics to articulate their insecurities. I've coached professors who suffer writer's block because they're terrified of being exposed: "I shouldn't have been given this promotion. When this book is published, everyone will understand why." I'm never sure whether it's reassuring that everyone is affected by imposter syndrome, or depressing that we're never free of it.

Pursuing a PhD can feel like a presumptuous pursuit. You're devoting a substantial chunk of time and money (perhaps somebody else's money) to an obscure area of human knowledge. Here are some common (and unhelpful) thoughts that we all experience:

This is pointless; nobody needs to know this stuff — By definition, a thesis *should* be obscure. You're making an *original* contribution to knowledge. And because you're pursuing depth, it has to be focused on a niche area. It might feel small,

2 As is often mentioned, it's not a syndrome at all. However, I'm using this term because it's widely used and recognised.

but you're making a contribution to a wider field, and you're an important part of that bigger picture.

Everyone else is much cleverer than me — I don't need to tell you that we tend to judge our *interior* against everyone else's *exterior*. That super-confident person delivering an insightful paper from the conference podium? You didn't see her shaking in the toilets beforehand. That elegantly-written journal article? How many drafts did he write? How much input did he receive from peer reviewers, editors, and proofreaders?

I'm going to fail! — By some miracle, I haven't yet been exposed. But they'll confront me at the viva and tell me it's all rubbish. This was playing in an endless loop throughout my PhD. At times, it was deafening. Eventually, I realised it was completely hindering my progress and that I had to get through it. I told myself that it *was* rubbish, but I was going to finish the wretched thesis anyway, *then* see what happened. *I was going to write a rubbish thesis.* As it happened, I passed with just a few typos to correct. Releasing some of that pressure (which was all self-imposed, I might add), allowed me to get on with it.

Imposter Syndrome, then, is just a means of self-protection. By never attempting anything difficult, we reduce the risk of failure. But you're an intelligent person with an exciting research project — surely the only failure would be in not trying? Now that we've established that Imposter Syndrome is here to stay, how do we manage it?

Defeating Your Inner Critic

We'll discuss writer's block and other maladies later, but now let's investigate that voice inside your head. The one that says, "who do you think you are to do a PhD?" "You'll never be able to finish it — remember that essay-writing contest when you were seven?" It might be uncomfortable, but we need to dwell on that voice for a moment. Really think about it. Now I'd like you to imagine who this inner critic might be. Describe the *sound* of their voice. Is it booming/querulous/squeaky? And what about their appearance? Are they a wizened version of you? A critical teacher? An unforgiving parent? The more precise you are, the better. You need to really get acquainted with this tyrant. If you like, write a description or draw a picture.

Once you've visualised them, you can square up and confront them. What could you say to this person?

> I'm not putting up with this shit any more. As you well know, I'm a successful academic researcher and more than capable of completing my thesis. I realise you're not going anywhere, but I'm ignoring you. I've got stuff to do here.

And poof! they're gone. Well, not gone completely. But you know how to deal with them if they pop up again.

If you're still struggling, you might need a more systematic approach. It starts with ABCDE.

Learning Your ABCDE

Most of us start out with good intentions to get some writing done. Then we hear the unwelcome voice of our Inner Critic: "You're not really a writer" ... "Who on earth are you, anyway?" ... "Have you seen the state of the kitchen floor?" Sometimes this adversary can be silenced with a chocolate biscuit, but often we need some hard evidence.

ABCDE is a tool developed by Professor Martin Seligman, one of the founders of the Positive Psychology movement, who based it on Albert Ellis' ABC model. Seligman's books *Authentic Happiness* and *Learned Optimism* are indispensable for unpicking the stories we tell ourselves and how they affect our lives.

Here's how you might use ABCDE to overcome your thesis block:

A is for ADVERSITY – Consider the situation you're in right now and describe it in as much detail as possible. But here's the thing: you have to do so using only facts. So, it's OK to say, "I didn't get any writing done today," or "I missed my deadline," but not "I'm too useless to do a PhD."

B is for BELIEFS – What did the situation say to you? Did it confirm any long-held beliefs, such as "I'm not really a writer," "I simply don't have time"? Look out for any absolutes, e.g. "I *never* get anything done," or "This *always* happens".

C is for CONSEQUENCES – How did that make you feel? And what were the consequences? Did you abandon all hope of getting anything done and eat a family size bag of Doritos instead? Note, these are the consequences of your *beliefs* and not of the situation. If you're familiar with Cognitive Behavioural Therapy (CBT), you'll probably know that our thoughts cause feelings that then determine our actions. Once we're aware of what's going on up there, we can intervene.

D is for DISPUTE – We're not going to sit back and take this nonsense – it's time to deploy some data. I don't know you, but I'm willing to bet you've achieved a great deal in your life. This is unlikely to be the first time you've attempted a piece of writing. What's your track record? Did you successfully complete a Masters' dissertation or submit a journal article? If not, there will be other comparable achievements that seemed impossible at the time, yet you conquered them. It shouldn't take you long to establish that those Beliefs above just aren't true.

E is for ENERGISE – Next, reflect on how you're feeling now. What's happened to your mood? Can you see any solutions that were invisible in that pit of despair? Are you ready to get going again in the knowledge that this thesis challenge is entirely within your capabilities? The Inner Critic won't necessarily go away, but you'll be able to vanquish it in moments by reminding yourself of previous achievements.

This exercise is especially useful if you write down your responses. It's then easy for you to whip out the document in difficult times. Although it can take a matter of moments for our mood to slump, it can just as quickly move in the opposite direction. In short, trust the evidence, not your emotions.

You can download an ABCDE worksheet from the website: www.howtofinishyourphd.com.

An Important Note

I want to acknowledge some of the limitations and criticisms of positive psychology. Over the last few years, some employers and universities have started offering (or insisting on) resilience training. Using techniques such as AB-CDE, they place all the responsibility for wellbeing on the individual, completing absolving the institution. The underlying message is: "We can treat you however we like, you just need to be more resilient." This is unacceptable. If you're being mistreated or affected by factors outside your control, it's absolutely not a case of simply adopting a positive mental attitude — the problem itself must be addressed. When major difficulties arise in the supervisory relationship, for example, they should be tackled directly. I give examples and proposed solutions in Chapter 4.

Furthermore, ABCDE, or other CBT-related exercises, are unlikely to be effective if you've been diagnosed with a mental health condition, such as depression or anxiety. Again, you need to treat the underlying issue first. Once that's under control, then these techniques might help manage minor fluctuations. I'll talk more about mental health in Chapter 5.

In short, then, exercises like ABCDE can be effective in situations where *you* are in control — for example, your writing habits. In Chapter 5, we'll consider what those situations might be.

Conclusion

As you can see, completing a PhD is not just an intellectual challenge — much of it is psychological, too. You need to thoroughly understand yourself and what's getting in your way. In Chapter 7, we'll explore how to build processes to consistently defeat that inner critic and other unhelpful voices. We can't stop it happening, but we can find better ways of managing those saboteurs. It's all about self-compassion, not self-blame.

We get so focussed on the problem, we catastrophise and are overwhelmed by the hideousness of it all. In this mindset, we can't come up with creative solutions. Worrying can feel constructive — we're thinking about our PhD — but it's not getting us any further forward. And we put *so much* energy into that worrying. Imagine how much you'd get done if you could channel that worry into action?

What I need from you now is a *commitment* to do

things differently. What got you to this point might not be enough to get you to the end of your PhD. Throughout this book, I'll be encouraging you to experiment with different techniques and approaches, some of which will feel uncomfortable or counter-intuitive. If these areas seem daunting, don't worry, I'll guide you through everything. For the moment, I just want to prepare you for change.

ACTION POINTS

» What are you going to stop doing? And what will you *start* doing instead?

» Identify the stories you're telling yourself. Are they helping? If not, could you replace them with better stories?

» If you're currently struggling with a specific problem, use the ABCDE worksheet to shift your thinking.

....

SUMMARY

....

» Focus on the present, which you can control, and forget the past. It's all about what you're going to do *now*.

» The stories you tell yourself affect your feelings and your actions.

» You don't need superpowers, just a willingness to persevere, learn, and develop a growth mindset.

Now that you're mentally prepared, we can create a plan.

....

TROUBLESHOOTING

....

There's no way I can change. I don't have the time or headspace. I'll have to keep going, exactly as I am.

This is a common predicament. Most of us fear change. It means doing things differently, which impacts upon how we behave and how we're perceived by those around us. That can challenge our sense of self. Also, we think that changing tactics will slow us down. Yes, it does initially, but then you'll *accelerate* once you have a better way of doing things. This is sometimes referred to as 'sharpening the axe'. If you're going to fell a large tree, you need to spend some time preparing your tools and thinking how best to approach it. Otherwise, you'll be hacking away to little effect and exhaust yourself. And the squirrels will laugh at you.

I often see PhD students who reach submission by clinging to old and efficient ways of working, but it always takes them longer. And they carry those ways of working to their next big project, too.

I really am too stupid to do a PhD

No, you're not. This belief shuts down your mind and prevents you from spotting solutions to problems. Tell yourself "I *can* do this, I'm just not there *yet*," and see what a difference it makes. Throughout the book, we'll explore many techniques for breaking it down and making it easier for yourself.

I can't make my inner critic shut up

This takes time. As I mentioned earlier, the inner critic never really goes away, but you'll get better at ignoring them. It doesn't matter what the voice is saying, you're going to get on with our thesis. Do try the ABCDE method. Evidence of previous achievements *proves* you're capable of finishing. Yes, a PhD is different from anything you've done before, but you're developing all the necessary skills. That *development* is part of the PhD.

3. Making a Plan

"The middle of every successful project looks like
a disaster." Rosabeth Moss Cantor

Now you've defined your purpose and prepared yourself
mentally, it's time to devise a plan. We all know that plans
seldom survive first contact with reality. However, having no
plan at all is the best way of ensuring that nothing ever happens. In this chapter, I'll be introducing you to the idea of
agile planning. That's not to say that your ideas or goals are
loose, rather you're keeping things flexible so you can adapt
when required. After all, there's no point in sticking to a plan
if you uncover a major issue that requires investigation.

Also, my mission is to help you break down your time
into more usable chunks or *sprints*. If you're partway through
your thesis, knowing you have a year left isn't helpful. What
does a year mean? And what needs to happen in that time?
It's hard to generate a sense of urgency when we imagine time
is abundant. When we think in shorter sprints and dedicate
them to specific activities, it's much easier to stay on track

and get a sense of progress. As David Allen explains in his phenomenally successful book *Getting Things Done*:

> [T]he real problem is a lack of clarity and definition about what the project really is, and what the associated next-action steps required are. Things rarely get stuck because of lack of time. They get stuck because the doing of them has not been defined.

Consider all the times when you make seamless progress on a project. Why was this different from your PhD? Probably because you had a clear sense of what needed to be done and when. Examples might include booking a big trip, getting married, or moving house. In this chapter, I'll help you develop a similar approach to your thesis. To do this, I want you to think like a project manager. This is *your* project. Then we'll look at who's on your team, decide what needs to happen and when, and anticipate some potential problems.

You're the Project Manager

One of the epiphanies I experienced during my PhD was that my thesis was just a project. As a former IT manager, I'd overseen dozens of projects, each involving a complicated mix of people, technology, and deadlines. This was no different. I had to manage resources, set milestones, and deal with things going wrong. *You* are the project manager of *your* thesis. Sometimes students think their supervisor is the project manager — perhaps because the supervisor presents themselves in this way — but it's *your* thesis. Even if your research is part of a larger project, you're responsible for your own contribution.

While your supervisor and institution have a vested interest in your successful completion, the person who's most affected is *you*. By taking responsibility for your PhD, you retain more control. So, you're the project manager. Like all project managers, you need to assemble a support team around you. Your supervisor should be on this team, of course, but it's not a symbiotic relationship. You need other people around you, too, who perform different roles.

We're going to focus on the supervisory relationship in the next chapter. For now, let's think about your team.

Who's on Your Team?

One of the strains on the supervisory relationship is when the student refers all queries and problems to their supervisor. From the student's point of view, this is much easier than asking more widely, and they see the supervisor's role as supporting them. The supervisor, meanwhile, grows increasingly frustrated. They're fielding questions about bibliographic referencing, conference funding, and theoretical frameworks. Although they probably know all this stuff, they're managing a full teaching load, pursuing their own research, supervising several other PhD students, and making a feeble attempt at a work/life balance.

You can reduce the strain on your supervisor (and therefore the relationship) by building a project team around you. Your supervisor is undoubtedly the right person to advise on your theoretical framework, but is there a workshop on bibliographic referencing or a contact in the graduate school who's responsible for funding? Your team might include colleagues, professional services staff, friends, family, even virtual networks. Your supervisor won't necessarily have the time or energy to provide moral support when you're flagging, so think about recruiting some cheerleaders.

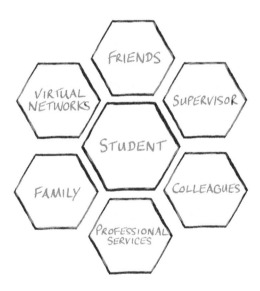

Most of my friends had only a very hazy idea about my research. That didn't matter. They asked me how it was going and reminded me this was an important goal. They cared about my success. Indeed, it might have been annoying if they'd started bombarding me with bright ideas about the thesis itself. Their enthusiasm propelled me through some dark periods.

It's important to note that some of your team members are giving their time voluntarily, so don't exhaust their goodwill. Also, university staff tend to be overstretched and will be limited in how much 1-2-1 time they can give you. When I run writing workshops, at least one attendee pops up afterwards to ask if I'll proofread their thesis. Firstly, I don't have time; secondly, I'm really terrible at proofreading.

Be reasonable in your requests and consider other people's priorities. As a project manager, you need to keep everyone motivated.

ACTIVITY

Who's on your team? Who will provide support with:

- » Regulatory issues?

- » Writing?

- » Accountability?

- » Encouragement?

- » Technical skills?

If you've written the same name next to every point, it's time to start thinking more widely.

What Needs to Happen and When?

In *The Seven Habits of Highly Effective People*, Stephen R. Covey3 asks us to 'begin with the end in mind'. Fortunately for you, your 'end' is clearly defined, and it's very much on your mind — you want to submit your thesis. If you're funded or approaching the maximum registration period, you'll have very little flexibility over when you finish. There's probably a date looming. While that might be scary, it's also helpful to have a deadline. Too much flexibility gives us the option of deferring tasks. First, we'll look at what needs to happen, then we can break it down into *sprints*.

Think about what needs to happen before your submission date. What are the steps you'll take? This might depend on the nature of your research project, but here are the typical steps.

» Research

» Completing chapters

» Production of a full draft

» Editing

» Incorporating feedback from supervisor(s)

» Final edits

3 Covey had nine children, so was clearly highly effective in all areas of his life.

» Formatting

» Proofreading

» Printing & binding

» Submission

How much time do you need for each of those steps? It's probably hard to know at the moment. By the end of this book, you should have a clearer sense of what's involved. If you're behind schedule, you might not have as much time as you'd like for every stage. For now, it's about creating awareness of the steps.

What else do you need to consider?

The steps where you need to be especially vigilant are those involving other people, such as getting feedback from your supervisor(s). Make sure you negotiate with them on a suitable date for sending a full draft of your thesis. Also agree on how quickly they'll respond. If you agree a deadline, make sure you honour it. Otherwise, your supervisor(s) might have other commitments and lack time to give your thesis the attention it deserves.

Other factors include:

» Work/teaching commitments

» Family responsibilities

» Holidays (yours and your supervisor's)

» Downtime (you can't work all the time)

» Significant deadlines (e.g. annual review)

» Conference papers/journal articles

Set some limits on PhD-related activities. There's probably no point in spending hours on teaching preparation if you're not interested in becoming a lecturer. And do you need to publish *during* your PhD? This might be essential for getting a job, but if journal articles are just a nice-to-have, they could slow down your thesis. Always consider the impact of any additional tasks. If you say yes to something else, you're saying no to your thesis. In Chapter 5, we'll look at other ways you can focus on your most important activities.

....

ACTIVITY

....

Have a go now at mapping out the remaining time for your PhD. There's no need to be precise at this stage — I'd just like you to get a sense of the time available and what you need to accomplish.

You can use any planning tool you like. There are some suggestions on the website: www.howtofinishyourphd.com. Or you can download a completion planner there, too.

I suspect that was a sobering exercise. Fear not, we're

going to work on your productivity and process and find some more effective ways of working. We'll also tackle any perfectionist tendencies.

Running out of time

Perhaps you've worked out your plan, and there simply isn't time to do everything before your deadline. If that's the case, you should seriously consider applying for an extension. It's much better to do this now, rather than the week when you're supposed to submit. I've worked with many PhD students in this situation who've suffered severe stress. Once we start panicking, our brain shuts down, and it's impossible to identify solutions. We also stop making any progress — all our attention is focused on the problem. Releasing some of that pressure is a huge relief and allows us to breathe once more.

In most cases I've seen, students who apply for a three-month extension actually submit within a few weeks of the original submission date. Once the pressure is off, they can focus on writing once more. Even if you don't go through with applying for an extension, familiarise yourself with the process — that'll make it less intimidating if you do need to apply. Most universities don't encourage extensions (they're keen on maintaining strong submission rates) so it won't necessarily be a straightforward exercise. You might have to negotiate and demonstrate that you have a plan for completion. This is worth doing, though, as it's in nobody's interests for you to give up.

While I'm being a wet blanket, I also want you to consider all the other things that could thwart you.

Anticipating and Mitigating Problems

As a catastrophist, I love anticipating problems. While I appreciate it's not everyone's cup of tea, at least *exploring* the idea of setbacks can help keep you on track. Once you've identified a potential mishap, you can devise a solution. It's much easier to deploy a pre-designed solution than to devise one when disaster has just struck.

Have a think about events that might hinder you over the remainder of your PhD. The nature of those events will depend on your research project and your personal circumstances. They could include:

» Change (or unavailability) of supervisor(s).

» Major life events, e.g. divorce/bereavement/moving house.

» Financial difficulties, e.g. running out of funding.

» Increased workload, e.g. if you're part-time or taking on teaching work.

» Data loss.

Is there anything you can do now to make it easier for yourself? In the case of financial difficulties, are there any emergency funds you could access? If you're concerned about the impending death of a loved one, what's the bereavement policy at your university? It would be worth alerting your supervisor to the situation so they can sign-post support. And please make sure you back up your thesis (and I don't mean by emailing it to yourself). There are some software recommendations on the website.

You can use this template for contingency planning. (There's a downloadable version available at www.howtofinishyourphd.com.

» What could go wrong?

» How could I prevent it?

» How could I fix it?

» Who could help me?

It's not much fun contemplating some of this stuff, but you could make things a lot easier for your future self. Anticipating difficulties makes them *less* rather than more likely to happen as you'll be more alert to the warning signs.

Breaking it Down into Sprints

The idea of 'writing a thesis' suggests you sit at your computer, then all those ideas are disgorged onto the screen in a continuous stream. Instead of 'writing a thesis', I want you to think in terms of a *series of actions* that finally produce a thesis. It's only by breaking it down that it becomes manageable. Once you have your overall plan in place, it's time to break it down further. We're going to create lots of milestones to keep you motivated.

I'm hoping you have at least three months before submission,[4] as we're going to break down your plan into 12-week sprints. Don't worry if this sounds athletic, it's not. The idea is that you *keep moving*. Consider for a moment: what sounds longer, three months or twelve weeks?[5] When we have the illusion of time, we tend to dawdle. Even saying something is happening *next month* suggests it's far in the future.

Telling ourselves we have a year to complete a project is fatal. We don't start, imagining that it'll be *much* easier to get going in the spring when it's lighter in the evenings. Then it's summer, and you're away on holiday or enjoying yourself. Autumn — that's a great time to start! Except lots is happening on campus. But wait, there's the Christmas break — it'll be very quiet. Yes, very quiet, apart from all the family commitments and parties. And can you really squeeze a year's work into a December fortnight? No. It might be the most magical time of year, but you won't suddenly produce 20,000 words.

We need to use what Brian P. Moran and Michael Lennington call the 12-Week Year.[6] Treating each quarter as though it's a full year ensures we maintain a lively momentum and set meaningful milestones. As they explain in their book,

....

4 If you have less than three months left, please read the Troubleshooting section at the end of this chapter.

5 Pedant's Corner: Yes, I know technically three months is a couple of days longer, but you get the point.

6 They don't hyphenate 12-week, so I'm passively-aggressively correcting it here.

the deadline is always near enough that you can't lose sight of it. We're going to make every day, week, and month count: no more wormholes, rabbit holes, or any other strange vortices.

....
ACTIVITY
....

OK, take the first three months on your annual planner. We're going to focus on what needs to happen during this period. Don't think about the rest of it at the moment. Another advantage of the 12-week sprint is that we don't allow ourselves to be overwhelmed by the entire project, we only concern ourselves with what's happening during *this* sprint.

Ideally, we're looking for three headline goals for this sprint. Depending on your stage, they could be:

» Finish reading for chapter 3.

» Draft chapter 3.

» Revise chapter 3.

Or ...

» Check thesis structure.

» Improve flow.

» Check references.

These goals are big but also specific. It shouldn't say "write some stuff".

Now we're going to break it down further. What's going to happen *each week*?

» Completing specific readings?

» Drafting, revising, editing specific sections.

» Completing specific activities, e.g. proofreading.

There's bound to be some slippage with this plan, but mapping your weeks in this way gives you a sense of how everything needs to fit into the sprint. If you're mostly hitting these weekly goals, you'll know you're on track.

You can download a 12-week sprint worksheet at www.howtofinishyourphd.com.

Don't go into any more detail now. In later chapters, I'll help you find time in your week to accomplish these goals. At the moment, it's probably like trying to fit an elephant into a ballgown. It might feel uncomfortably tight. Perhaps you'll need to lower your standards, limit your scope, or find a way of working more efficiently. That's what we'll consider in Chapters 5, 6, and 7.

What are the hurdles?

We anticipated some potential problems a moment ago. Now think more specifically about hurdles that might arise during this first sprint.

Looking at your 12-week sprint, consider:

» What hurdles can you anticipate?

» How could you *avoid* those obstacles through advance planning?

» If there's nothing you can do in advance, how might you deal with these obstacles when they pop up?

The specific hurdles depend on your circumstances, but here are some examples.

Parenting responsibilities

If your sprint coincides with the school holidays, realistically, you're unlikely to get much time to yourself. You'll get frustrated, and the children will sense your frustration. Everyone's grumpy. Accept that this needs to be a break for you (at least from your PhD) and start your sprint afterwards. Or perhaps lower your expectations and ringfence a small amount of time each day. Maybe you can negotiate childcare or take it in turns with other parents, so you at least get a couple of afternoons to yourself.

Work commitments

Combining a PhD with paid work is tough, especially if it's a role with a lot of responsibility and fluctuating workloads. Thanks to COVID-19, it might be much easier for you to work from home now. This might help you set stricter limits on your working hours and get more done. Avoiding a commute and chatty colleagues could really boost your productivity.

It perhaps feels scary to change your work patterns, but you could just try it for this first 12-week sprint and see how it goes. Hopefully, some of the prioritisation and productivity tips in the later chapters will help you with your work, too. I found the good habits I developed during the final stages of my PhD also transformed my working practices.

Is there any flexibility in your job? Could you work a compressed week? This typically involves completing all your hours in four days rather than five or getting a day off every other week. You're still doing the same amount of work, but having an extra day that's just for your PhD could make all the difference. For this to be effective, you need to completely ignore your work email and firmly decline meeting requests on those days. If you've accrued a lot of annual leave, could you use this to schedule some regular PhD days?

Having a life

There's nothing worse than the sound of other people enjoying themselves, especially when we're stuck indoors writing.

In the UK, we only get three days of truly good weather each year, so you're unlikely to be missing *that* much. If you're feeling sorry for yourself, imagine the thousands of other PhD students around the world who are in precisely the same position. Seek solidarity with your invisible comrades.

If you're determined to scamper about in the sunshine, get your work done as quickly as possible. I'll show you how in Chapters 5, 6, and 7. Unless you can make your thesis a priority, you'll be missing many more summers. You need to be clear on your priorities and have the courage to say no to distractions.

Once you've mapped out your first sprint, discuss it with a friend, partner, or supervisor. This provides a helpful reality check and also commits you to action. When your 12-week sprint is complete, you can reflect on how it went. I'd suggest using the thirteenth week to review your results and plan the *next* 12-week sprint. An *entire* week might seem indulgent, but dedicating this time helps you make the most of your next sprint. This is also an opportunity to discuss progress with your supervisor or accountability partner and take a short break.

Conclusion

As a project manager, you're responsible for managing your resources. One of those critical resources is time — the hours, days, and weeks available to you. Thinking in smaller units or sprints helps us make better use of them. Unless we pay attention, entire months can slip by where progress is imperceptible to the naked eye. Sometimes we get stuck in fantasyland, where we imagine that we'll definitely get going *next week*, without actually creating the conditions for progress to happen. If we want a different outcome, we need to do things differently. And we need a plan.

A good plan gets you started and shows you where you're going. The process (which we'll create later) ensures that you're getting things done every day and you're paying attention to those milestones. Even if problems do arise — and they *will* — you'll be better placed to assess the impact on your plan and make the necessary adjustments. That plan should be adaptable.

You also need to think about who's on your team. While a PhD is famously a solo effort, you still need a supporting cast. Who else could help you? Relying on your supervisor for everything can cause frustrations and is also likely to slow you down. In the next chapter, we'll look at how you can optimise the supervisory relationship so it's both professional and productive.

ACTION POINTS

» Work out what needs to be done over the remainder of your PhD.

» Anticipate problems and devise solutions.

» Decide who's on your project team and assign roles.

» Plan your first 12-week sprint.

SUMMARY

» You are the project manager for your PhD.

» You need to assemble a project team to support you.

» Anticipating problems makes them less, rather than more, likely to happen.

» Breaking down your project into sprints makes it more manageable.

TROUBLESHOOTING

I've created my plan, but there's just not enough time to do everything.

OK, here's what you can do:

» Have you been too generous in allocating time for certain tasks? Could you squeeze them a bit more? Are you setting your standards too high? Consider each step critically and see whether it could be shortened or simplified.

» Consider an extension. As I mentioned earlier, giving yourself extra time reduces pressure, and you might not even need it.

» Do less. Is everything strictly necessary? Take another look at the earlier section on Setting Limits. You just need to do enough for the examination process — your thesis is part of an exam, it's not a book!

If you don't have enough time left for a 12-week sprint, plan a shorter sprint. The key is to break down the available time into smaller chunks that you manage more effectively, then assign specific chunks to each day and week.

I've identified a critical problem, but I'm not sure what to do about it.

Talk to someone. Think back to your project team. Is there somebody who's been through a similar experience? If not, anybody who is good at listening will help. Often, we just need to talk through our options. As I mentioned earlier, we tend to get so focused on the problem that we lose the ability to identify solutions. There's *always* a solution.

I have no idea how long everything will take

Talk to colleagues who've recently finished their PhD. Although their experience won't be identical to yours, they can tell you the stages that took longer than anticipated. Once you've completed the later chapters in this book, you'll also have a better idea of how much time you'll need for editing.

It's impossible to predict exactly how long you'll need. The point of planning is to give yourself some structure and milestones. They can be adjusted as you go along. As you progress through your PhD, you'll get quicker anyway — both because you'll have a better sense of the project and because the impending deadline will motivate you. Nobody ever believes me when I say this, but it's true. There's nothing more motivating than the sudden realisation that soon you could get your life back.

4. Working with Your Supervisor

"The single biggest problem in communication is the illusion that it has taken place." George Bernard Shaw

Like any relationship, the supervisory relationship requires effort and compromise. Even if it's exciting at first, there comes the point where you have to decide who's going to empty the bins. Also, the supervisory relationship needs to shift as you make the transition from student to independent researcher. Problems occur when either the student wants to remain dependent, or the supervisor is keen to exert too much control.

As you're the project manager, it's up to you to manage the resources available to you, and this includes your supervisor. That's not to say that you get to boss them around — it's a matter of establishing the best way of working together. Equally, they're not *your* boss, either. Although they'll have an idea of the milestones for your PhD, they're not involved in what you do each day. They aren't there to manage you or to answer every question.

In this chapter, we'll explore the role of the supervisor so you can work out what you need from then at this stage of your PhD. We'll look at getting the most from your supervisory meetings, soliciting the right sort of feedback, and agreeing your completion plans. Occasionally, supervisory relationships break down, so we'll identify some potential causes of conflict and consider a few solutions — with the help of a vampire and a superhero.

Adapting the Supervisory Role

By the end of your PhD, you'll be an independent researcher. Over the last few years, you've been developing all the necessary skills that you then demonstrate through your thesis and viva. Although you won't be as experienced as your examiners, you *will* be an expert in your specific niche. It's a big shift to go from thinking of yourself as a student to becoming an expert, but it's a necessary one if you're going to make and defend that original contribution to knowledge.

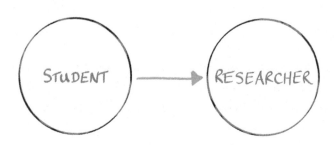

For your independence to grow, your supervisor needs to give you more freedom. That also means you need to take more responsibility. I've adapted the model below from the Hersey-Blanchard Model of Situational Leadership to show how the supervisory relationship might develop throughout your PhD.

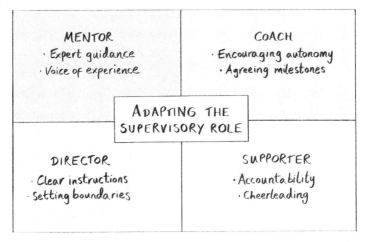

Director — at the beginning, you need clear direction to get on the right path. Your supervisor is also setting boundaries for the working relationship and agreeing expectations.

Mentor — once you've orientated yourself, they need to give you more latitude. Your supervisor remains the voice of experience (e.g. "You can't read *everything* that was ever published on this topic. I know, because I tried"), but you should be allowed to make your own mistakes (unless it's a health and safety issue). Your supervisor should also prompt you on critical milestones, such as applying for ethical approval, and make sure you understand what's involved.

Coach — by the time you've gained some momentum, you should become more independent — e.g. making your own decisions and finding solutions to problems. Your supervisor provides encouragement by flagging milestones and agreeing priorities, but they're no longer *directing* you. Coaches help clients to harness their own inner resources — they don't tell them the answers.

Supporter — in the final year of their PhD, you're an expert on your research project, even if your supervisor knows more about the wider context. You're preparing to defend a thesis and need to take full responsibility for it. Your supervisor isn't part of the examination process.

Inevitably, this is a simple model, and doctoral progression is seldom straightforward. However, the ability to adapt your role is vital. You might need to revert to an earlier role, for example, if you return after a long absence or suffer a crisis; you should then adapt again when the time is right.

As a PhD student, you must learn to:

»   solve problems

»   overcome obstacles

»   trust your own judgement

»   develop confidence

»   become independent

Is your supervisor allowing you to do so? If not, you might need to *demonstrate* that you can do all these things.

Think about where you are on this model, and also where you *should* be. If you think your supervisor is trapping you in the wrong quadrant, it's time for a chat. Ask them where they think you should be at this stage. If you're not quite there, what needs to happen? Ultimately, your supervisor is successful if you no longer need them (you might want to find a diplomatic way of telling them that).

The supervisor's role is often implicit — it's assumed that both they and you understand their responsibilities, even though those responsibilities aren't fully documented. While they're not *trying* to obstruct you, the lack of clarity around the role means they sometimes unwittingly place obstacles in your way. Often this is due to a lack of communication. By taking the initiative in managing the supervisory relationship, you can ensure that expectations are both explicit and reasonable.

Managing the Supervisory Relationship

Yes, it's up to you to manage the relationship — especially during the final stages of the PhD. You need to work out what you need from your supervisor and then negotiate an agreement. They might be unable to provide the support you want, so then it's a case of reaching a compromise.

Some areas to discuss include:

» How will you communicate? Is email appropriate? How quickly does your supervisor think they can respond?

» Who sets the deadlines? Are they going to prod you, or are they expecting you to motivate yourself?

» When will you meet? Do you need more frequent, shorter meetings? Or brief Skype/Zoom chats to check you're on track?

» In what format will you submit work? Are they expecting something polished, or are they happy with a rough draft?

» What sort of feedback do you require? If you're still working on early drafts, you'd probably appreciate guidance on the arguments and structure; anyone who's a couple of months from submission really doesn't want to hear about an exciting new methodology. We'll look at feedback in more detail at the end of the chapter.

You also need to make the most of those supervisory meetings. Creating an agenda in advance means there's no danger of forgetting an important issue or getting lost in a chat about pets, children, and holidays. We hope that supervisors are giving the meeting some thought in advance. In reality, though, they'll suddenly get an Outlook reminder and shout: "Arrggh, who am I seeing and what's their topic?" You should take responsibility for those meetings. You can download a sample Meeting Agenda template from the website: www.howtofinishyourphd.com.

Areas you could include are:

What you've done since the last meeting – especially updates on agreed actions.

Questions or difficulties – anything that proved challenging or confusing.

Feedback – discuss any feedback you've received on written work. Perhaps you need clarification on specific points.

Agreed actions before next meeting – what you're going to work on next. Your supervisor can then confirm that this is the next priority.

Organising yourself in this way signals to your supervisor that you're a capable researcher. They're likely to feel more relaxed about you acting independently and won't interfere. It also means you feel in control. This is vital for a project manager.

....
ACTIVITY
....

Create or adapt a meeting agenda template for your supervisory sessions. You might need a couple of versions — one for routine meetings and another for more significant reviews.

Dealing with Multiple Supervisors

Even when there's a supervisory team comprising several academics, inevitably much of the load tends to fall on one of the members. Some supervisors create an aura of unhelpfulness so they don't have to deal with routine matters. Unfortunately, too, female supervisors are sometimes seen as responsible for pastoral issues, and students are less likely to 'bother' a male supervisor.

In areas where you're expecting supervisory input, who's the best person? You don't want two or three different people advising on methodology or theory. It's highly unlikely that they'll all agree and you could end up stuck in the middle. Could you get your supervisors to agree on different areas of responsibility? Ultimately, this is less work for them and provides greater clarity for you.

Dealing with Conflict

Most supervisory relationships remain positive and constructive throughout. Occasionally, though, problems arise that demand significant effort to achieve a resolution. Here, we'll look in more detail at some potentially difficult situations and consider some approaches you might take.

Developed by Stephen Karpman, the Drama Triangle offers a social model of human interaction. Specifically, it describes the connection between personal responsibility and power in conflicts, revealing the shifting and often destructive roles people play. These unhelpful behaviours occur in many situations, including the supervisory relationship.

The three potential roles in the Drama Triangle are:

The Victim – the victim feels oppressed, helpless, and powerless. This leaves them unable to make decisions, solve problems, or achieve any insight into the situation. Everything is the fault of external circumstances and other people.

The Rescuer – the rescuer loves nothing better than to swoop in and save the day like a superhero. Although they are trying to help, this behaviour actually keeps the Victim in a state of dependency. The Rescuer, meanwhile, can ignore their own needs by focusing entirely on "saving" somebody else. So, this can lead to an avoidance of their own problems, disguised as concern for the Victim.

The Persecutor – the persecutor is critical, controlling, and inflexible. They give feedback that keeps the Victim in a state of helplessness. This role might appear authoritative, but it arises from an unwillingness or inability to address underlying problems. They drain their Victim's life force.

You can probably see how these roles might emerge in the supervisory relationship. If the student decides to be the Victim, it's very easy for the supervisor to rise up as either the Rescuer or the Persecutor. Neither role is helpful! The supervisor can end up as the Victim, too. Insecure students might become Persecutors, making unreasonable demands and refusing to accept feedback.

If you find yourself in a supervisory relationship that isn't working, consider what's happening on the Drama Triangle. Have you or your supervisor adopted a specific role, forcing the other one into another unhelpful behaviour?

Common scenarios include:

Student as Victim – the student is overwhelmed by the challenge of pursuing a PhD and expects everyone else to help them. This results in a state of learned helplessness, where they don't actually develop the necessary skills. The supervisor is required to spend considerable time and effort keeping them going, often to no avail.

Supervisor as Victim – the supervisor is overwhelmed by the challenge of supervising a student, either because it's their first time, or due to a heavy workload. The student doesn't get the support they need and falls behind.

Student as Rescuer – with a supervisor who is a victim, the student sometimes tries to save the day by overlooking missed appointments or trying not to take up too much time.

Supervisor as Rescuer – with a student in a state of victimhood, the supervisor repeatedly solves their problems, making them feel better and avoiding the underlying issues.

Student as Persecutor – the student, perhaps aware of their own limitations, blames the supervisor and makes them responsible for everything. All solutions are external, requiring more time and resources. Whatever is provided is never enough.

Supervisor as Persecutor – lacking the skills or the time to achieve a lasting solution, the supervisor becomes more demanding in the hope that the application of pressure improves performance.

Can you spot any familiar patterns here? It's easy to fall into these roles, in any areas of our life or work. When the supervisor becomes a Persecutor, the automatic response is to become a Victim. This serves only to perpetuate the roles. Of course, you can't tell your supervisor they're a vampire who's draining your life-force. What you need instead is to achieve a Win-Win.

Reaching a Win-Win

You might have come across the idea of achieving a Win-Win in a situation, and this maps quite neatly with the Drama Triangle.

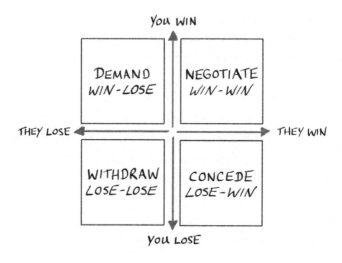

If you make an unreasonable *demand* on your supervisor, you become a Persecutor. Although you might win in the short term because they become a Victim or Rescuer and concede to you, it's not going to be an effective long-term solution. They'll probably feel resentful and might then also become a Persecutor. Then you have a vampire battle on your hands.

If you *concede* to an unreasonable supervisor, this resolves the conflict very quickly — but also temporarily. This just shifts the problem to the future. You could then end up having to address it when you're close to submitting your thesis.

In some cases, both student and supervisor *withdraw*. Neither relishes the idea of conflict or the awkwardness of a difficult conversation. The student then stops making progress, and this is bad for everyone.

Where you want to be, then, is in the top right quadrant, the *win-win*. Here you negotiate a resolution that's best for both you and your supervisor. You need support, they need a student who successfully completes. It's in everyone's interests to find an effective way of working together.

Arrange a meeting with your supervisor to discuss how you're going to work together. This session is purely to work on your *relationship*, not on the thesis. Try to reach a compromise on the areas outlined in the section on *Managing the Supervisory Relationship*. Sometimes supervisors don't realise students have many competing priorities and therefore make unrealistic demands on them. Equally, students can forget that supervisors have ridiculously heavy workloads. They'd love to give you more time, but it's impossible.

Changing Supervisor

If you've made an effort to resolve conflict yet the problems persist, it might be time to consider changing supervisor. I appreciate this is disruptive, but a destructive relationship could stand in the way of you finishing your PhD. Changing supervisors isn't that uncommon, although obviously universities don't like to talk about it. Here's how you might go about it:

1. First, talk to somebody impartial. It's always helpful to get another perspective. Perhaps there's a counsellor on campus, a Student Union representative, or a colleague who'd agree to a confidential chat. Sometimes just talking through a problem with a good listener helps us identify a solution.

2. Consider who might be a good alternative supervisor. The process is likely to be a lot smoother if you already have somebody in mind. This could be your second or third supervisor or somebody else in your department. Ask around (discreetly) to find out what they're like. You don't want to replace one Persecutor with another! Ideally, you should approach them to find out whether they'd be happy to take you on. Consider, though, that they might say something to your current supervisor, especially if they're friends.

3. If it's not too awkward, speak to your current supervisor and explain why you want to change. Make your PhD the focus, not the personalities, e.g. "I think it would be better for my project because X is more familiar with my methodology," or "I believe Y has more time to give me the input I need at this stage." Assuming your supervisor has also found the relationship difficult, they might be relieved. Then you've achieved that much-coveted Win-Win.

4. The appointment of supervisors is usually managed by a central research student office. There should be information on their webpages outlining the process, along with the forms that need to be completed. You probably have a Director of Graduate Studies (or similar) in your school. They typically approve the change. If your supervisory relationship has broken down completely, you should go straight to this Director. In the unfortunate event that your supervisor is also the Director, speak to the research student office. This will have happened before.

5. Be persistent. University procedures take time, and

it could be many months before the change is officially approved. In the meantime, think about what you could achieve. Are there areas you can work on that don't require significant supervisory input?

Discussing Plans with Your Supervisor

Once you've formulated a completion plan, you should discuss it with your supervisor. You'll need their support to execute it. Perhaps this involves them playing a different role, giving you more input, or changing the way you work together. They should be involved in the planning stage, as it affects them too.

Show them your overall plan and 12-week sprint. Do they think it's realistic? Can they suggest any key milestones you need to be aware of, such as an Intention to Submit process? Does your supervisor have any commitments that could affect your plan? You might be hoping to send them a full draft just as they head off for a sabbatical or big research trip.

The final stages of your PhD are stressful for both you *and* your supervisor. They sometimes feel as though they're also being judged during the examination process. In a few cases, this can provoke unhelpful interventions, including:

» Suggesting a delay to submission.

» Expressing a lack of confidence in the project.

» Insisting on perfection or impossibly high standards.

» Recommending significant changes at a late stage.

» Requesting changes to changes already agreed.

Of course, they might have legitimate concerns, but you should always discuss their suggestions rather than accept them unquestioningly. Here are a few outlines of how you might approach the potential problems outlined above.

Suggesting a delay to submission

This sometimes happens when a supervisor hasn't noticed how much progress you've made, especially if you've suddenly accelerated. Listen to their concerns, then show them how you've planned your time. Demonstrate that you've considered everything that needs to happen and have also allowed some contingency. If your plan isn't realistic, then it's their job to question you.

Expressing a lack of confidence in the project

This is unacceptable, especially if it's the first time they've expressed reservations. Firstly, tell them how this makes you feel. This is awkward, I realise, but they need to understand the impact of their words. They're focusing on the thesis and forgetting the person behind it. Then request constructive feedback on their *specific* reservations. What do you need to address? Which are critical issues? Are any nice-to-haves, but not strictly necessary? Are they going to make the difference between a pass and a fail?

Insisting on perfection or impossibly high standards

There's no such thing as a perfect thesis! Ask them if they're thinking of the PhD as a book rather than an examination. In any case, 90% of candidates are given corrections. If you feel comfortable in doing so, gently point out that the examiners' idea of perfection will differ from theirs.

Recommending significant changes at a late stage

Explain the consequences of making such a big change. Ask whether it's really going to make the difference between passing or failing your viva. After all, there's always a chance that your examiners would prefer the original version.

Requesting changes to changes already agreed

This is the sign of a supervisor who is either nervous or unable to spend much time providing feedback. Calmly explain that you've already implemented their changes (a paper or email trail is helpful) and ask why further changes are now necessary.

These last few problems can often be prevented by being specific on the type of feedback you need.

Soliciting Constructive Feedback

Providing constructive feedback is the most essential part of the supervisory role. It's also the part that seems to cause the most problems. You can make life easier for everyone by making sure you're asking for the right sort of feedback, in the right format, at the right time.

What sort of feedback do you need?

In the early stages, you're seeking high-level input on the structure and arguments — the absolute fundamentals of your thesis. It's not helpful for someone to point out all the small grammatical errors on something that's likely to be re-worked multiple times. Equally, when you reach that elusive final draft, you won't be too pleased if someone suggests an entirely different structure or new ideas.

First, then, consider what stage you're at and what input you need:

» Structure?

» Arguments?

» Flow?

» Style?

» Grammar and spelling?

Who's the right person to give you this feedback? For structure and arguments, it probably needs to be one of your supervisors. When it comes to flow, style, and tiny details, though, you don't necessarily need a specialist in your field. In fact, it might be better if it's someone who *doesn't* know anything about your subject. A researcher in a *related* field will be smart enough to grasp the general direction of what you're doing, but they won't come up with any conflicting ideas about how you should completely change it. Instead, they're likely to focus on the *clarity* of your writing.

How to ask for feedback from your supervisor

Make sure you're explicit when requesting feedback. For example:

"This is an *outline* of my argument. I need to know whether it's convincing and logical."

"This is an early draft of a chapter. I'd like feedback on the structure and flow. I'll be addressing the writing style later."

"This is my fourth draft. I've finalised the structure and flow, but I need your thoughts on whether the writing style is clear."

Also specify the format of the feedback. Do you want your supervisor to edit your Word document and track changes? This approach is effective mainly if you want them to look at smaller details. When soliciting feedback on overall structure and argument, this approach might tempt your supervisor to start correcting your spelling. Perhaps instead you could ask for a couple of paragraphs in a separate document.

Another alternative is a spoken commentary. Feedback

often feels uncomfortable because it's impersonal. We can't see the person's facial expressions or hear their tone, so we assume they're angry with us. Would your supervisors either agree to a Zoom chat where you can share the document, or record a voice memo for you? This is probably quicker for them than typing out their feedback, too.

By being clear on exactly what you require, you improve the chances of your supervisor getting it back to you quickly.

Implementing Feedback

Does this sound familiar? The long-awaited email lands in your inbox — it's the feedback on that piece of writing. Your stomach ends up in your slippers, and you feel slightly clammy. You open the document and start reading. Disaster! Your supervisor clearly hates this piece of work. It's a sea of red comments, and they're all negative. There's no choice but to start all over again. This is complete rubbish. You spend the next couple of hours fuming and wondering why on earth you ever started a PhD. You complain to anyone who has the misfortune to ask you how it's going today.

Later on, you take another peek at that feedback. Having calmed down, you spot a positive comment, even the occasional "this is good". Those comments that seemed to demand a complete rewrite are just indicating that a sentence needs to be tweaked. "Hmm," you think, "this isn't quite as bad as I thought." Feeling slightly foolish, you start working through the comments and realise that some of them are making your work much better.

Although I try to be rational, this is my reaction every time I receive feedback. Mind you, my excuse is that I'm a Victorianist, so I'm *supposed* to be melodramatic. There's not much I can do to suppress that initial wave of negativity, but I then quickly follow up with a systematic process for assessing and implementing that feedback. *Reviewing* is the crucial stage that many of us forget when we're wallowing in a pit of despair.

Reviewing Feedback

Read through everything slowly and carefully. Start making notes, keeping any positive comments at the top — this helps you maintain that growth mindset. Flag anything unclear, for instance, if you don't understand what your supervisor is asking/suggesting, or you don't know how to implement it. You want to be clear on what you're doing before you start. If there's a vague comment such as "This needs to sound more academic," ask your supervisor for clarification.

You're not asking them to copy-edit your writing, but to give just one example that you can use to meet that standard. This could be an extract from someone else's work or a strong paragraph from your own writing. You can then use this as an anchor point. Maybe they just need to suggest the sort of terminology they'd expect to see. They should illustrate the gap between where you are now and where they expect you to be.

Once you're clear on what's required, you can get going. While it might feel efficient to start at the beginning and work your way through comment-by-comment, this is often much harder. Maybe there are a few quick wins at the beginning — correcting some typos or finding a better word — then suddenly there's a bigger task, such as finding some additional literature. Even worse, a later comment perhaps suggests we delete that whole section we just carefully tweaked. We thought we were flying, now there's no hope of getting it finished today. This is why you need to *triage* your feedback.

Triaging Feedback

First, sort your feedback into large, medium, and small tasks. I've put them in that order for a reason. You want to tackle the big issues first, as they'll probably relate to structure and argument. Then you can move on to medium-sized tasks, such as improving the flow. Finally, you tackle the smaller details. You don't want to be spending your time on stuff you're going to delete later.

Triaging your feedback in this way:

» Avoids duplication of effort.

» Gives you a more realistic idea of how long it's going to take.

» Allows you to batch tasks.

It's much better to correct all your citations in one go than to intersperse this rather tedious activity alongside other bigger tasks. You'll build some momentum and probably find a better way of doing it.

Assessing Feedback

You also want to decide *whether* to implement that feedback. Feedback is essentially data — some of it is good, some is bad, some is just indifferent. If you're in the final stages of your PhD, you should be the expert on your particular niche. Although your supervisor will have more experience in the wider field, they haven't spent as much time with your data and probably haven't read exactly the same literature. They're dipping in and out of your project alongside dozens of other commitments.

Unfortunately, supervisors don't always have time to read everything more than once, and they might have forgotten earlier discussions about why you've done something in a certain way. A common issue is when a supervisor's feedback states "You need to add X…", whereas feedback on an earlier draft said, "You need to delete X…" (or vice versa). This tells us three things:

» There's often no right answer.

» Supervisors are human and therefore fallible.

» We need to trust our own judgement.

You need feedback to be as objective as possible. If three different people give you three different suggestions, then this is just opinion rather than fact. Indeed, if the same person gives you three different suggestions at different times, it's plain unhelpful. In the absence of consensus, you get to exercise your own judgement. If something is factually wrong, then, of course, you need to change it, but if someone offers a different *opinion*, it's time for you to decide.

You're the person who will be defending this thesis. It's much easier to defend a decision you've made yourself. Whereas you should always *consider* your supervisor's feedback, you shouldn't necessarily always implement it. Their suggestion might have been based on a quick glance at your draft when they didn't have time to think back to previous discussions.

If you do find yourself in this situation, here's what you can do:

» Flag any feedback you disagree with, then contact your supervisor to request clarification.

» If appropriate, you can alert them to any documented previous discussions, e.g. comments in earlier drafts, previous email threads, your supervisory meeting notes (if you're required to keep them by your university).

» Ask them whether making the requested change would mean the difference between a pass and a fail. If it's going to take you a whole week and not affect the outcome of your viva, is it really worth it?

You don't need to do this triumphantly as though you've caught them out. Instead, just point out the conflicting suggestions, state your preferred option, and ask them to confirm your choice.

Remember:

» Feedback helps you grow as a writer.

» It's faster and more effective than trying to work out those problems for yourself.

» Feedback isn't always right! You're an academic researcher, so apply your critical judgement to feedback, too.

Your Feedback Strategy

» Get into the right mindset *before* you open that email — take a deep breath.

» Assess what needs to be done.

» Clarify any ambiguities or disagreements with your supervisor.

» Triage the feedback into large, medium, and small.

» Develop an implementation plan and add it to a sprint.

Conclusion

Maintaining a harmonious supervisory relationship can be pivotal to your PhD success. Like any relationship, though, it can deteriorate when unhelpful assumptions persist. Think about what you need from your supervisors and whether that's realistic. If problems do occur, that's not a reflection of you or your project — it's more likely to be down to a mismatch, unmanageable workloads, or other stresses.

Students can end up in the role of victim or persecutor because they don't have enough people around them. Your supervisor can't give you support in every area of your life and PhD, even if they want to. Make sure you build your project team. And as project manager, take responsibility for optimising the supervisory relationship by planning meetings, improving communication, and raising issues before they become intractable problems.

By taking more responsibility, you also build your autonomy — an essential part of your transition towards becoming an independent researcher. The harder your supervisor works on providing a solution, the less effective they'll be! You'll be far more committed to a solution you've devised, too. Managing your workload can reduce some of the pressure on the supervisory relationship. That's what we'll do in the next chapter.

ACTION POINTS

»   Think about what you need from the supervisory rela-
    tionship *at this stage*.

»   Arrange a session with your supervisor(s) to discuss
    completion plans and what you need from them.

»   Create or adapt a meeting agenda template for your
    supervisory sessions.

SUMMARY

»   The supervisory role needs to adapt so you can become
    an independent researcher.

»   Take the initiative in planning supervisory meetings
    and finding more effective ways of working together.

»   Deal with any problems as soon as they arise.

»   Make sure you're asking for the right sort of feedback
    at the right time. And assess it critically.

....

TROUBLESHOOTING

....

My supervisor keeps giving me the wrong sort of feedback

Sometimes supervisors will go through and correct all your spelling and grammar, but completely ignore your argument. This usually happens because they're so distracted by the errors that they can't focus on the argument. It's hard to look at structure, flow, *and* details simultaneously. You'll see why in Chapter 8.

You can avoid this scenario by making sure your draft is clean. As I'll explain in Chapter 6, you shouldn't be spending too much time tweaking at this stage, but you should definitely run it through a spellchecker and make sure it's tidy before sending to your supervisor. Explain that you'll be checking the final version thoroughly. For now, you need their expert opinion on the soundness of your argument.

My supervisors never agree

Dealing with sparring supervisors can feel as though you're stuck between divorcing parents. They both want you to take their side, and you feel peculiarly responsible for the whole situation. Although you realise the importance of remaining neutral, it can then become impossible to make any progress on your PhD.

This is a delicate situation, but one that can be resolved

with some diplomacy. The fastest way to resolve any conflict is to establish a point on which everyone can agree. In this case, that should be the importance of you finishing your thesis. Even if your supervisor secretly believes that them being right takes precedence, they hopefully won't articulate that thought (if they do, it's definitely time to replace them). It's in nobody's interest for you to fail or not complete.

Having agreed the common goal, describe the current situation and how it's getting in the way of your work. You can acknowledge that they each have strong views and want what's best for you, but it doesn't help when they're permanently in conflict. You're caught in the middle and don't know which way to turn. Suggest that they agree to take responsibility for specific areas of your project, e.g. methodology, theory, writing style, or progress. This has the added advantage of reducing their workload. There's a lot of wasted effort if multiple supervisors are arguing about your theoretical framework.

Ultimately, it's your thesis, and you'll be defending it at your viva. Make sure you're making decisions that are right for you, rather than just keeping the peace.

I'm having problems with my supervisor, but it's too late to change

If you're within six months of completion, it would be too disruptive to change. Work out the absolute minimum you need from your supervisor — this might be just reading a full draft and providing their signature on your submission forms. Is this possible? If not, perhaps there's another academic in your department who could give you some feedback on your draft? Although they can't formally replace your supervisor, they might be willing to give you a chunk of time to help you reach the finish line.

You could also speak to your Director of Graduate Studies. They'll have encountered this problem before and can help come up with a solution. It's their responsibility to help you.

5. Managing Competing Priorities

"Eventually everyone sits down to a banquet of consequences." Robert Louis Stevenson

If you haven't made much progress on your thesis, it's possibly because you're letting everything else take priority. That's certainly what happened to me. It would feature on my to-do list each day, but would always get bounced to the next day, and the next, and the next ... I'd be delighted if a client emailed me with a request. Even if it wasn't urgent, I would treat it as such — this was the perfect excuse to ignore my PhD for a bit longer. Your thesis must be a priority at least *most* of the time.

Often, it's about inclination — what we *feel* like doing. We avoid a good habit because it's not very enjoyable. But it's not always about having fun. If I go to the gym intending to enjoy myself, I fail nearly every time. However, if my objective is to improve my strength and fitness, I *succeed every time*. Occasionally I enjoy myself – if, for example, a poseur walks into a mirror – but mostly it's a slog. But that (almost) daily effort will hopefully keep me vertical and mobile for another four or five decades.

It's the same with academic writing. Few of us enjoy the process, but we crave the recognition or outcomes that it brings. Don't think about whether you want to write, think about whether you want the *rewards*. This could be either your graduation ceremony, a specific job, or the satisfaction of having finished. If you did the exercise in Chapter 1, you'll have a handy list to remind yourself why you want to get this done. Unless we can *see* those reasons, it's far too easy for us to forget that this is a priority.

First, we'll establish what's truly within your control and focus on *now*, not what's happened in the past. Then we'll survey all those competing priorities and work out how you can make sure you're pursuing the right activities each day. Often, this involves saying no, something that's hard for most of us. As I'll explain, the secret to finishing your PhD isn't lots of completely uninterrupted writing days, it's establishing smallish blocks of time and then protecting them. We'll also discuss the importance of looking after your health. Pushing yourself too hard is counterproductive and short-lived. What you need is *sustainable* progress.

Your Circle of Control

At the moment, it's easy to think there's very little that's within our control. Unfortunately, we're right. However, this makes it even more important to focus on what we *can* control. In *The Seven Habits of Highly Effective People*, Stephen R. Covey separates our lives into three concentric circles: control, concern, and influence. The Circle of Control includes events we control directly. In the Circle of Influence, we find those areas where we have some control but are also partly affected by the behaviour of other people. Finally, the Circle of Concern is everything that affects us, yet we're powerless to change it. When I use the exercise with students, this outer circle is usually inhabited by Brexit, parents-in-law, and spiteful weather.

ACTIVITY

Draw three concentric circles on a piece of paper or download a template from www.howtofinishyourphd.com.

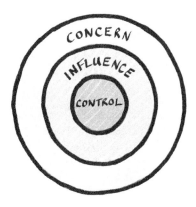

Scribble down what you believe is within your Circle of Control. What can you actually direct each day (barring accidents and emergencies)?

Next, consider what lives in your Circle of Influence. So, these are factors over which you have *some* control, but routinely require negotiation with other people. This could be the relationship with your supervisor, family dynamics, or managing paid work.

Finally, look at your Circle of Concern. This is generally intractable stuff that distracts or annoys us, but we can't actually do anything about it. Typically, this might be world events or university regulations.

As you'll see, the Circle of Control is minuscule – perhaps the size of a 10p coin. But there's enough space for a few tiny actions. And tiny actions, over time, build up into significant results. Writing 500 words a day doesn't feel like much, but after a month, you'd have 10,000 words. Yes, really! Even if there are only 30 minutes a day that you truly control, I'd like you to focus on how you can make the most of it. Zoom in on that 10p coin and ignore the rest.

A Note on Time Travel

"I try to take one day at a time, but sometimes
several days attack me at once." Ashleigh
Brilliant

The only way we can hope to influence the future is by making the best use of today. What we do each day determines, at least in part, what happens in the coming weeks, months, and years. The trouble with being human is that we do a lot of time travel. Either we're despairing about what happened yesterday, or catastrophising about what *might* happen tomorrow. All that worry prevents us from concentrating today and doing our best work. We unleash a flock of what Charles Darwin called the wibber-gibbers, feathery creatures that surround us with self-doubt and prevent us from making progress.

As Dale Carnegie explains in *How to Stop Worrying and Start Living*:

> [T]he best possible way to prepare for tomorrow is to concentrate with all your intelligence, all your enthusiasm, on doing today's work superbly today. That is the only possible way you can prepare for the future.

Carnegie's delightfully sexist analogy is that his wife doesn't mind washing the dishes because she washes only one day's dishes at a time. She's not trying to wash yesterday's and tomorrow's all at once. We can't possibly cope with the burden of the past and the future and also hope to function today. Focus instead on today and do your very best. And if you're watching your wife wash the dishes, grab a tea towel and help.

Any demanding regime, whether it be a diet, exercise, or writing, can falter when we try to control the future. How am I going to achieve my goal next week, or next month?

But if we decide, "today I'll write 500 words" and do our very best to achieve it, we can reset the counter and try again tomorrow. We have no control over what's going to happen then. Maybe something else will get in the way, maybe you'll write 1,000 words. It's impossible to know. Start your morning with "*Today* I'm going to ....".

Although we often begin with good intentions, it's easy to get derailed by competing priorities. Let's tackle those now.

Managing Your Time

> "There is usually an inverse proportion between how much something is on your mind and how much it's getting done." David Allen, *Getting Things Done*

Everybody is busy. If you're stuck in the middle of your PhD, it's not because you haven't been working hard. I suspect it's because you're busy with other stuff. It's the difference between getting things done and getting the *right* things done. It's absolutely vital to focus on what's truly important *now*. I'm not suggesting that your other activities aren't necessary, rather that some of them need to temporarily take a back seat. As I mentioned in the introduction, your thesis absolutely has to appear consistently at the top of your to-do list. It's time to rethink your priorities.

One of my favourite tools for reality checks is the Eisenhower Matrix, popularised by Stephen R. Covey. You might've seen it pinned to office walls. Here's what it looks like:

Quadrant 1 — Urgent and important. Here's where you'll place those tasks with a screaming deadline and unexpected emergencies, such as illnesses or broken boilers.

Quadrant 2 — Important but not urgent. This is the spot for tasks that are crucial to you but haven't yet become stressful. You routinely feel in control of these activities. By keeping on top of them, you prevent bigger problems occurring in future.

Quadrant 3 — Urgent but not important. Typically, I think of this as Other People's Shit. They've decided that I should do something urgently, but it's not actually *my* priority. I'm too busy having a crisis in Quadrant 1. If you're teaching, this could include unreasonable last-minute requests from students, e.g. "I need you to explain the Harvard citation style in the next 5 minutes."

Quadrant 4 — Not urgent and not important. Why do

we spend any time here at all? Well, usually it's because we're trying to avoid tasks in Quadrants 1 or 2. These often involve watching kitten videos on YouTube, faffing about on Twitter, or shopping for matching stationery.

....
ACTIVITY
....

Have a go at adding your own tasks to the quadrants. Use a big piece of paper so you have room to include everything.

When that's done, reflect on the following points:

» How does stuff end up in Q1?

» How could I spend more time in Q2?

» How can I better manage the tasks in Q3?

» Can I stop (or at least limit) things in Q4?

When I use the matrix in workshops, attendees often put their writing in Quadrant 1. Although this sometimes happens despite our best efforts, your life will run more smoothly if you're mainly inhabiting Q2. You're working on important tasks, but they haven't turned into mini-crises. The trouble with letting stuff slip into Q1 is that you have no wriggle room when disaster strikes, those illnesses and broken boilers demand your full attention. If you've left that writing dead-line to the last possible moment *and* your boiler explodes, you have two emergencies on your hands. It's much better to develop a steady writing schedule (and get that boiler serviced).

I also see people add exercise, cooking, and socialising to Q4. Your health absolutely belongs in Q2 — this includes both your mental and physical health. If either breaks down, you can't easily fix it. Don't let it become an emergency. I'll talk more about this later in the chapter. While partying every night won't get your thesis finished, neglecting relationships completely can leave you isolated and without a support network. Partners and family members are part of your project team, too, so it's essential to keep them on side. Housework is also a popular Q4 activity. I'm generally inclined to agree, as it's not much fun. However, some chores might belong in Q2, such as laundry. After all, you don't want to have to go to the library in your dressing gown.

Have you ever reached the end of a busy day and realised that you've achieved none of your priorities? Sometimes, we get buffeted around solving everyone else's problems and neglecting our own. This makes us feel good about ourselves, but we don't make progress on what's important to *us*. We're particularly susceptible to this situation in shared workspaces. There's always someone having a crisis. If this is a problem for you, could you work somewhere else? Getting trapped in Q3 is just an insidious form of procrastination. We become helpful elves, always ready to attend to everyone else's priorities.

The Eisenhower Matrix is an ongoing activity. You'll need to revisit it at least weekly to reassess the situation and see what's shifted. It might be necessary to reprioritise and use stricter criteria, especially if you're up against a tight deadline. Ask yourself:

» What can I delegate/outsource? (if you have an income, this might include takeaways, childcare, or cleaning).

» What can I postpone?

» What can I drop?

Remember, the only way you'll finish your thesis is by saying no to distractions and honouring commitments to yourself.

Saying No

> "It's only by saying 'no' that you can concentrate
> on the things that are really important." Steve
> Jobs

Saying no is hard, I realise. It took me a long time to perfect this skill, but now I actually enjoy it. Not in a sadistic way, but because it makes me feel that I'm taking my priorities seriously. Yes, I'd love to be the sort of person who could solve everyone else's problems, but I'd much rather be someone who commits to meaningful projects and delivers them successfully.

Here are my tips on saying no:

» Never agree to anything immediately — say you need to check your diary (this gives you valuable pondering time).

» Think about whether it's actually good for *you*.

» Consider what impact it'll have on your priorities/timescales (take a look at your 12-week sprint).

» Set some limits, e.g. I'll help you for an hour, then I have an appointment.

» Don't get a reputation for being good at something you hate!

If the answer is 'no', tell them quickly so they can find someone else or a different solution. People who regularly make cheeky requests are used to rejection, so don't feel as though you're letting them down.

Now, one of the problems of being a PhD researcher is that you're confronted with many opportunities, some of them more attractive than others. A few senior academics like to harness your energy for tasks such as conference organisation and teaching. While this can provide useful experience in some cases, often it's a time-suck that threatens your schedule. Remember Quadrant 3?

If you definitely want to teach after graduation, then it's worth investing time in getting relevant experience; if you're planning to leave academia, it probably isn't. Anyone who's done teaching will know that it involves a lot of extra hoof-work in the shape of marking, email, and tutorials. Nobody explains precisely what's involved and it's too late once you've realised.

Learn to value your own time as highly as other people's. If you say yes to something else, you're saying no to your thesis. Only do so when it's truly important. By protecting your Q2, you have the time, energy, and focus to manage those priorities. Part of this is ensuring you have blocks of time for writing.

Choosing the Best Time to Write

The critical decision you need to make now is *when* you're going to write. Assuming you have a choice, of course. If you have caring responsibilities, there might be a fixed slot when you can write, e.g. at night when the children have gone to sleep, or early in the morning, before they're vertical again. Otherwise, there's probably some flexibility in your schedule.

If you're a morning person and trying to get your writing done in the evening, you could be making life unnecessarily difficult for yourself. Can you swap your tasks around to maximise your energy? Are you doing something in the mornings that doesn't require much brainpower? Likewise, can you nocturnal types keep a few evenings free?

I write best in the mornings. I wouldn't describe myself as a lark — that suggests perkiness — but I'm just better with more creative tasks before midday. I can often return to the task later in the afternoon, but only after I've made a strong start. The heavy-lifting needs to be done when I'm fully alert. My absolute peak is 9.00-11.00, so I try to avoid scheduling routine stuff during those hours. I can achieve more in this slot that I can in the rest of the day.

....

ACTIVITY

....

Have a think about your own day. Are there any points at which you feel especially productive? If so, can you protect them?

Finding Time in a Busy Schedule

I sometimes work with part-time PhD students who combine research with a full-time job and rearing tiny children. They explain their punishing schedule to me and point out that they can't possibly squeeze in any writing. Unfortunately, there's no other way of getting a PhD. Nobody is going to award you a doctorate based on your *potential* to write a thesis. The solution usually involves making some tough choices:

» Asking to reduce work hours.

» Taking a sabbatical.

» Negotiating with a partner or family member to take more responsibility for childcare.

> » Getting up earlier and writing before anyone else is awake.

> » Postponing the PhD until you have more time.

The last option is unappealing, but you won't get a different outcome unless the circumstances change.

I don't have children, but have coached many parents. The answer is nearly always to work early in the morning or late at night, depending on what suits you best. And not being available to your family *all* the time. The benefits to them might not be obvious. However, you'll be a much happier parent/spouse if you finish your PhD and enjoy that sense of achievement. Explain to them why this is important to you. Some PhDing parents feel as though they're being selfish. No, you're actually modelling an excellent example of what can be achieved through hard work and perseverance. Agree times when you'll be fully engaged with family activities and clearly communicate when it's time for your PhD. This might involve politely but firmly reminding household members of those agreements.

....

ACTIVITY

....

I'd like you to print a weekly planner or use a diary for this one. You can also download a template from the website: www.howtofinishyourphd.com. I think it works better as a paper-based activity, but it's fine to use your usual calendar software. The challenge here is to block out some periods for writing during your week. They need to be *scheduled* in the same way as any other commitment, such as a meeting or a seminar. If other people have access to your online calendar, mark it as a private appointment. Unfortunately, colleagues, students, or family members might think your writing time is negotiable.

1. Block out your immovable commitments, e.g. paid work, medical appointments, family responsibilities. Don't forget to factor in travel time (unless you have a seat on public transport, you can't get much done when you're in transit).

2. Now schedule some writing sessions. Don't be too overzealous at first. Setting yourself an ambitious target then failing to meet it is a shortcut to despondency. Maybe schedule a couple of two-hour stints during the week and see how that feels. Was it easily achievable? Great, now you can add some more or extend those sessions. Perhaps it was a stretch? How about revisiting your Eisenhower Matrix and moving some other commitments into Q3 or Q4? Or could you start with a couple of one-hour sessions?

3. Add in some buffers for mundane tasks, such as email and admin. When I'm working on a big project, I always imagine this stuff will somehow get done without my allocating any time. I then get frustrated because it's eating into the hours when I'm supposed to be creative. Anticipating and allowing for these activities is good for lowering stress levels.

4. Allow yourself some fun. You can't be working at

capacity *all* the time. Scheduled downtime provides an opportunity to recover your energy and enthusiasm.

5. Don't fill every waking moment. Unless you're one of those ruthlessly efficient people, you'll soon feel as though you no longer have any control over your life. Even self-imposed regimes can become stifling. Make sure you've covered the priorities, and then cut yourself some slack.

If you can't get your week to work on paper, it won't work in reality. When I relax at the weekend, my brain quickly fills with all sorts of exciting ideas for the following week. When I try to fit them into my planner, I realise I'd need a 300-hour week to get even half of it done. Even the scientists among you can't defy the laws of physics.

Weekly Review

Try this schedule for a week. How did it go? Were you able to stick to those slots? If not, what happened? Were there some Q1 events, i.e. genuine emergencies? Or could they perhaps fall into Q3 or Q4 instead? Think carefully before cancelling those writing sessions. If you can't commit to your PhD, how will you finish it? Would you cancel any other commitment for this reason?

What's the *cost* of not setting or protecting those periods for writing? It could be a financial cost, such as paying additional fees, or perhaps the emotional cost of added stress or frustration. Missing one or two sessions won't be disastrous, but this has a compounding effect over time. What we need instead is the compounding effect of *good* habits, as we'll see in Chapters 6 and 7.

We'll come back to *how* you use those writing sessions in the next chapter. For now, we're just establishing it as a priority — that's all you have to do.

Prioritising Your Health

"Fanaticism consists of redoubling your efforts
when you have forgotten your aim." George
Santayana

I can't be sure, but I *suspect* you've created an ambitious schedule for yourself earlier. Did you include any downtime? If not, please go back and add some free periods. Not only do you need time to recharge, but this also provides contingency. Don't be tempted to push yourself too hard. A punishing schedule over a sustained period leads only to exhaustion. You might get ahead briefly, but then you're out of action for weeks. A realistic schedule, pursued consistently is more effective than frantic bursts of activity.

One of the reasons why I suffered a massive slump in the middle of my PhD was exhaustion. During the first year, I pushed myself incredibly hard. My progress would've been astonishing for a full-time student, but I also had a job. Although I got away with the pace initially, it simply wasn't sustainable. I started to get frustrated when the next phase was so much slower. I'd spend ridiculously long sessions at my desk, resulting in searing back pain and agonising sciatica.

Morphine certainly didn't help my mental acuity. Looking after your mind and body yields many benefits.

There aren't many depictions of a PhD viva in film, and probably for a good reason. One notable example is *The Theory of Everything*, a biopic of the late Professor Stephen Hawking. Apart from it being a good story, there are a couple of things to learn from Hawking's experience. Firstly, his examiners aren't convinced by *all* of his thesis. Although he became one of the greatest scientists of his generation, parts of his thesis were ropey. Secondly, Hawking enjoyed a social life. Although he occasionally pulled all-nighters, this was the exception rather than the rule.

I'm typing this section during a weekend writing retreat at a UK university. We're putting in long hours, arriving at 9am and leaving at 8pm. Yet other people are here when we arrive and remain rooted to the spot when we're having our dinner: the PhD students. When I mentioned to the caretaker that there were still people in the building, he said: "That's fine, I can lock up — they won't be leaving." Working when you're exhausted produces terrible results. Then you work even later to fix the problems and probably just make them worse. It's a vicious circle. Cutting back on sleep is absolutely not the way to finish your thesis. When we're tired, we lose the ability to see the situation realistically. While we need a little bit of pressure to keep us going, too much produces the opposite results.

The Human Function Curve

Originally created by cardiologist Dr Peter Nixon, the Human Function Curve shows the link between pressure and performance. As pressure increases, so does performance, but only up to the point where the pressure becomes too great. Then performance starts to dip slowly before plummeting.

On the left-hand side, where there is little pressure, performance is correspondingly low. In the context of a PhD supervisory relationship, this might indicate that we lack autonomy or a clear sense of what's required from us.

Moving across, the next section represents the **comfort zone** where we understand what needs to be done and also possess the resources to pursue those objectives. Within the comfort zone, greater pressure can actually improve performance.

As the pressure increases, we reach the **stretch zone**. Here, we feel less confident but are motivated by the additional pressure. This is where we often achieve optimum performance, as we're overcoming challenges and developing our research skills.

If we're not careful, we slip into the **strain zone**. This is where the pressure exceeds our ability to cope. The dotted line represents the fantasy that our performance will continue to improve, regardless of the pressure. However, in this strain zone, our performance *decreases*. The typical response is to work even harder in the hope of pushing through the zone

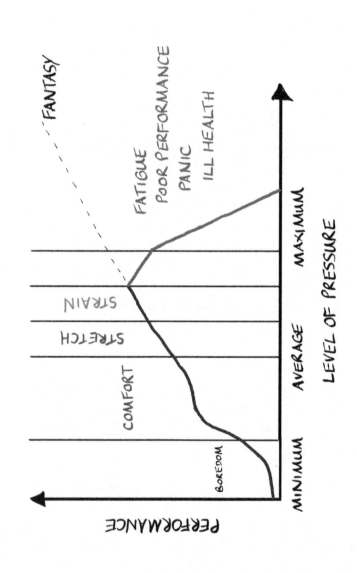

into the realms of fantasy.

Working harder often involves sleeping less, avoiding friends and family, and neglecting physical health. This, naturally, further impacts upon our ability to cope with the situation. Once we become *distressed*, we're in danger of intermission or actually giving up our PhD altogether. I recently coached a late-stage PhD student who had taken up permanent residence in the fantasy zone. Repeatedly working late into the night, he made lots of mistakes — such as accidentally deleting all his citations — and then he had to work even longer to fix them all. Soon he was sleeping only two hours a night and falling out with his family. His health suffered, and it very nearly killed him.

This curve maps the *typical* zones, but everyone is different. Someone who is dealing with existing mental health problems is likely to reach the strain zone more quickly.

. . . .
ACTIVITY
. . . .

» Where do you think you are currently on the Human Function Curve?

» How might you recognise the signs that you're strained rather than stretched?

» What steps could you take to protect yourself?

If you're already in the strain zone, you must seek help right away. You might not feel comfortable discussing mental health with your supervisor, but perhaps there's a counselling service available at your university or some local support services. Please don't keep plunging into the fantasy zone. You'll find some links to support in the Resources section.

You are your most valuable asset, and you need to look after yourself.

Looking After Your Mental Health

Over the last 10 years, there has been a fivefold increase in the number of students disclosing depression to their university.[7] However, just under half of students who receive treatment for mental health problems choose *not* to inform the institution. This means we don't know the true extent of the problem, which makes it even harder to tackle.

One of the barriers to acknowledging the current mental health crisis is that pursuing a PhD is *supposed* to be stressful. It's almost a badge of honour to be working around the clock, skipping meals, and losing friends. While stress is a normal part of our lives and difficult to avoid, the problems occur when it becomes *di*stress. *Stress* is time-limited and doesn't usually interfere with our ability to complete daily activities. *Distress*, however, is much longer lasting and prevents us from functioning normally. It might also be accompanied

....
7 Thorley, Craig, *Not by Degrees: Improving Student Mental Health in the UK's Universities* (London: Institute for Public Policy Research, September 2017), p. 3.

by other negative emotions, such as feelings of worthlessness.

As I'm not the useful sort of doctor, I'm not qualified to offer advice on mental health. I can, however, write from experience. I suffered chronic depression for many years then two particularly debilitating episodes, one of which fell plum in the middle of my PhD. There's lots of well-meaning advice out there about maintaining a balanced diet and exercising regularly. Annoyingly, this *does* help. Nevertheless, when you're in a pit of despair, it's very hard to practice self-care. If you're struggling to even have a shower in the morning, you probably won't feel motivated to take a 5K run and then prepare a healthy dinner from scratch.

Get some external help first. This could be either talking therapy, medication, or both. Not everyone wants to take anti-depressants, which is entirely understandable, but the right prescription in combination with other supports can help. Once you feel more in control, you're in a much better place to make lifestyle changes. Then it becomes a virtuous circle. You need to get out of that hole before you can look around and see the possibilities rather than just the problems.

When we're not feeling robust, thinking we should be doing all that other stuff becomes yet another way of beating ourselves up — it's *my fault* for not starting the day with two hours of yoga and fermenting my own yoghurt. Don't let anyone tell you than seeking support is a form of weakness. Quite the reverse. Strong people show their vulnerability and allow others to help them.

Conclusion

If you can't manage your time, it's almost impossible to finish your thesis. Although we think the answer is an empty schedule for writing, that's not the reality for most of us. Stipulating unrealistic conditions is simply another form of procrastination — as if we needed another one. It's not about having as much time as possible, it's making the best use of what you've got. That's what we'll do in the next chapter.

You'll never complete your thesis if you can't make it a priority at least some of the time. Obviously, there are many other compelling priorities, too, but your writing can't always languish at the bottom of the to-do list. Making commitments to yourself and consistently honouring them is the secret to PhD success. Prioritisation is about doing the important stuff, even if we don't feel like it. We need to be effective rather than efficient. Spending time in Q3 *feels* productive, but we're serving someone else's priorities. And don't just tick things off a list. Once you combine intentionality with effort, you'll achieve remarkable results.

Although your PhD should take temporarily take precedence over lots of other activities, your health is always of prime importance. If you sacrifice your mental or physical health, it's much less likely that you'll finish, and you'll end up with problems that affect many other areas of your life, too. Don't get stuck in that Fantasy Zone. Small and consistent achievements are far more effective than writing frenzies that leave you exhausted. It's not about working harder, it's about working smarter.

ACTION POINTS

» Draw your Circle of Control and marvel at its tininess.

» Create an Eisenhower Matrix and assign your usual activities to one of the four quadrants.

» Identify blocks of time in your week for writing and consider what might get in the way.

» Add some downtime to your week.

» Take a look at the Human Function Curve and think about the signs that you might be strained rather than stretched.

SUMMARY

» Don't allow yourself to be overwhelmed by your Circle of Concern. Reading the news won't change anything — you'll just get sad. Focus instead on your Circle of Control.

» Think critically about your weekly activities. Are you routinely prioritising stuff that's getting in the way of your thesis? What could you drop?

» Protect some time for writing — every week. It doesn't have to be a lot, but it *does* need to be consistent and focused. Quality, not quantity.

» Your thesis needs to be a top priority, but your health is even more important.

....

TROUBLESHOOTING

....

I have too many competing priorities, I don't know where to start

There are a couple of approaches you can take:

1. Which of those priorities is the most stressful? Getting this one out of the way might help you relax and gain more headspace for those other tasks. Is there an activity that depends on someone else's support? If so, tackle this first to give them more time to provide some input. While they're doing their bit, you have an opportunity to work on something else. You could also pick the most appealing task. This is an easy win that gives you some motivation and momentum.

2. Pick one randomly! If they're all equally important, it doesn't matter where you start. The alternative is paralysis. Once you've decided what to prioritise, give it *all* your attention during the allotted time slot. Dissipating your attention and energy across multiple activities means only

ever making a tiny amount of progress in any of them. Big results require disproportionate effort.

I'm still distracted by my Circle of Concern and can't focus on anything.

This is understandable. It's hard enough doing a PhD under normal circumstances, let alone in the wake of a global pandemic and recession. However, excessive worry only makes the problem worse. If you're worried about getting a job after you graduate, you'll improve your chances significantly by completing that thesis. You can't control the economy or the job market, but you *can* control whether you do any writing today. Set yourself some tiny targets and build up gradually. It's hard to focus for a whole day when you're preoccupied, but you might be able to manage it for 30 minutes to start with. Over the next two chapters, we'll build a productive routine that's right for you.

I'm absolutely exhausted, but I must get my thesis finished.

I've seen so many PhD students in this position, especially those who also have jobs. They push themselves too hard and run the risk of losing everything. A posthumous PhD isn't nearly as much fun. One student was absolutely determined to pursue an unrealistic timeframe so she could apply for a postdoc. Eventually, she realised the likelihood of ending up with neither the postdoc nor the PhD. We came up with a more relaxed plan which didn't compromise her health. And she got a great job at the end. Had she worn herself to a husk, she would have performed poorly at both her viva and subsequent job interviews. Remember that Fantasy Zone. If you take a break, you'll be much more effective when you come back.

6. Becoming a More Productive Writer

> "The secret of getting ahead is getting started.
> The secret of getting started is breaking your
> complex overwhelming tasks into small
> manageable tasks, and then starting on the first
> one." Mark Twain

You've probably heard the advice: "treat your PhD like a job and work regular hours". This is so unhelpful and gets me really quite cross. I've met many students who obediently perch in front of their laptop in the shared workspace each morning, then knock off at 5.30. What happens during those hours? Absolutely nothing. Being present isn't enough. Academia is entirely in the grip of presenteeism — a culture that privileges appearance over reality. And what if you already have a job? Then this advice is useless. If you've ever worked in an office, you'll know that many employees spend relatively little time being productive. This is not a good analogy.

What we want is focused activity, and at the right time.

As I mentioned earlier, a plan shows you what you need to do, but executing it is another matter entirely. Once you've protected those time slots for writing, you have to use them *productively*. It's the *intentionality* that gets you to the goal. That's what we're going to explore now. Everyone's approach is completely different, so we can't just copy what our colleagues are doing. Developing a productive writing habit depends on your commitments, preferred working style, and personality.

In this chapter, we'll look more closely at that weekly plan you created earlier and create a *writing fortress* to defend it. You'll work out exactly what you're doing, when it's happening, and how you'll approach it. Finishing your thesis isn't about the number of hours spent at your desk, it's what you do with them. We're going to protect your writing time, develop a strategy for using it effectively, improve focus, create accountability, and defeat procrastination. Let's get *intentional*.

Revisiting Your Weekly Plan

Although we want some flexibility in our week, it's no good just deciding what we fancy doing every Monday morning. We'll either pick a displacement activity, go over something we've already revised endlessly, or just quietly despair — anything but tackle the most important task. You need a structure to ensure the important stuff gets done. If we only tackle what we *feel* like doing, the difficult tasks get consistently ignored. Reducing the number of decisions you make conserves energy and boosts momentum.

Remember that weekly plan from earlier? Now we're going to add some detail. You're not thinking about the whole 12-week sprint here — just that first week. By planning at this level, you'll start to see what's feasible. As project manager, you're giving yourself a clear structure that lets you know what should be happening and when.

Hopefully, you already identified a couple of blocks for writing. We'll come back to those in a moment. Look at the rest of the week. Although it might be full of other commitments, are there other gaps where you could squeeze in some less intensive work?

In *Getting Things Done*, David Allen explains four criteria for choosing actions:

» **Context** — e.g. location, equipment available.

» **Time available** — if it's just 5 minutes, this limits what you can do.

» **Energy available** — how mentally taxing is the proposed task?

» **Priority** — what results in the biggest payoff?

Context

If you need to take a one-hour train journey, is there anything you could achieve in this time? Is it possible to take a laptop? If not, could you edit a printed draft? When I worked at a university, I had a 12-minute train commute. You wouldn't think that's enough to achieve anything meaningful. Nevertheless, I'd often use it to write the opening sentences of a chapter. They're always the hardest and most time-consuming. If I tried to do this at home, I'd just keep re-reading what I'd already written. For these micro sessions, I'd take nothing but that first paragraph and focus on just one sentence.

Time available

You can't get much writing done in five minutes, but it's certainly long enough to check a few references. That type of systematic task is suited to short bursts, especially given it's quite dull. Unlike writing, there's no need to build up momentum or hold lots of information in your head. Conversely, if you do find yourself with an unexpectedly empty afternoon, could that be a good opportunity for sustained work on a problematic chapter?

Energy available

As we saw in the previous chapter, it's essential to identify our best hours for writing and make sure they're not occupied by non-priorities. Equally, we want to avoid pushing ourselves too hard at times that aren't right for us. If you're a morning person but have a couple of free evenings, find some less demanding activities to do then. Finishing your PhD isn't all about big ideas. Much of it involves organising material, which is something you can do when you're low-powered.

Priority

When you have competing priorities and it's not clear which you should confront first, consider which you *most want to finish*. That euphoria of having completed an unattractive task is motivating and also clears your mind. If you've forgotten your priorities, hop back to the previous chapter.

·················

ACTIVITY

·················

» Create a list of tasks you could accomplish in an odd 5-minute gap. Try to think of ten. Some of them will be terrible, but the more ideas you generate, the greater the likelihood of a few gems.

» Now think what you could do with a spare hour.

» If there's a priority that's been niggling at you, could you chip away at it in these moments?

Making good use of these short blocks of time can add up over the weeks and months. It's like putting all your 50ps in a jar — it doesn't look like much at first, but soon you have enough for some moderate fun.

Protecting Your Writing Time

It's all very well finding some time to write, but then you have to defend it — vigorously. You need a *writing fortress*. Tell somebody that you want to work uninterrupted for just 30 minutes, and it'll be a matter of moments before they insist on asking whether you fed the cats. If you wear headphones in a shared office, colleagues feel able to destroy your concentration so long as unnecessary questions are prefixed with "I know you're busy, but ..." The rules don't apply to them, because they're *special*.

You might have to hide yourself away where nobody can get you, or be prepared to communicate your needs firmly, clearly, and repeatedly. At home, nobody will ever say, "I thought you might like to get some writing done today, so I've cleared the kitchen table, done all the chores, and arranged to take the children out for the afternoon." You'll have to make your own time and ruthlessly patrol it. If you usually work from home, it might be necessary to remove yourself to a café. For those of you with teaching responsibilities, an off-campus location would be better, away from colleagues and students who might pester you with questions.

I once coached a group of researchers who were all struggling to get any writing done in their shared office. They spent much of the time interrupting each other and getting frustrated. Eventually, they agreed that the first two hours of each morning would be for focused work — whether that was writing, thinking, or reading. Those who craved a longer session arrived earlier, and those with short attention spans wandered off and bothered people in other offices. Although it took a little while for this to become an established routine, it proved hugely popular. The researchers could tackle their trickiest tasks during that session and make significant progress that would carry them through the rest of the day. Again, it's the *quality* of the time, rather than the quantity.

In *Zen in the Art of Writing*, American author Ray Bradbury explains how he produced the first draft of his best-selling novel *Fahrenheit 451* in just nine days. Finding himself unable to concentrate at home with small children, Bradbury escaped to the library at the University of California. There in the basement sat neat rows of typewriters that could be rented for a dime per half hour. You inserted your dime, the clock started ticking, then you had 30 minutes to hammer away at the keys. As an aspiring author, Bradbury had limited funds: "Time was indeed money."

With such tight restrictions in place, Bradbury had to think carefully about how he'd use those sessions. There was no way he could spend the first 20 minutes wondering what to write. Those decisions were all made in advance while he was doing chores at home. When he arrived in the basement, Bradbury was ready to get going. As he explains, he needed to be "a maniac at the keys". There was no way of getting more time, so he had to be highly effective in using the resources available to him. It's unlikely you can find a coin-operated typewriter, but in a moment we'll look at a couple of techniques for creating short bursts of focused activity.

....
ACTIVITY
....

How could you create a writing fortress?

This might involve:

» Taking yourself to an undisclosed location.

» Informing colleagues, friends, and family members that you'll only respond to genuine emergencies.

» Negotiating with people who interrupt you, e.g. agreeing a time when you'll help them with their query. They'll soon get fed up. This is a "not yet," rather than a "no". Although as we saw in the previous chapter, sometimes a flat "no" is required.

You'll need to be both firm and consistent. Once you've made an exception, this sets a precedent and your writing time is no longer sacrosanct. Now you've established your writing fortress, you need to know what you're going to do there.

Making Writing Easier for Yourself

"First you make a mess, then you clean it up."
William G. Perry Jr

I've run many writing workshops and retreats over the last 6 years, and also coached hundreds of individuals. The biggest obstacle I see is that the sufferer (for this is a serious condition) is trying to produce perfect prose — instantly. The words should spring fully formed from their minds onto the screen, else it means they're not a good writer. Writing should flow, yes? No! It should flow for the *reader*, but that's what editing is all about — and editing comes later. The writing *process* is seldom elegant.

How do we end up with this misconception? Well, I think there are a couple of reasons. Firstly, we compare our drafts with other writers' published works, works that have been professionally edited and proofread, and extensively revised by the author. We don't see the endless drafts or hear the impotent shouting when nothing seems to fit.

Secondly, nobody really talks about the challenge of writing. As academics, it's something we're just *supposed* to do. The fact that you're smart means it's a doddle to craft an 80,000-word argument. The higher you go in academia, the less acceptable you'll find it to discuss the difficulties of writing. I've had many conversations with professors who confide that they have absolutely no idea how to go about writing an article — it just somehow happens after months, sometimes years, of struggle and stress.

I find that most people need at least five stages to produce a finished piece of writing. I've experimented on myself and others, and this is broadly the approach that tends to work.

The Writing and Editing Cycle

Zero Draft – a loose and sketchy collection of ideas, just for you! You absolutely don't share this with anybody else. Pick out the good ideas and develop them in the …

First Draft – here there's some attempt at structure, but the main aim is to develop your ideas without worrying about how everything fits together. Then you're ready for the …

Second Draft – now you're refining those ideas, thinking about and strengthening your argument, dropping anything that doesn't fit. You're starting to consider your reader and perhaps sharing it with your supervisor or trusted friend. With their input, you move on to the …

Third Draft – this is where you're clarifying, improving consistency, signposting and implementing any feedback. Once this is done, you proceed to the …

Final Draft – only now do you address the tiny details, such as whether that should be a semi-colon or a dash. Proofreading is unbelievably tedious, so you don't want to spend time perfecting drafts that are still changing.

You might need fewer or more steps. If you're a scientist, you might be writing in a more structured way from the outset, as there are usually strong conventions that need to be followed. For those of you writing in a more exploratory way, you'll probably find it easier to apply structure retrospectively. This way, you're not inhibiting yourself. Whatever your approach, you need to break it down into stages. There's no such thing as writing efficiently. Consider this quote from writer Anne Lamott in *Bird by Bird*:

> Shitty First Drafts. All good writers write them. That is how they end up with good second drafts and terrific third drafts. I know some very great writers, writers you love who write beautifully and have made a great deal of money, and not one of them sits down routinely feeling wildly enthusiastic and confident. Not one of them writes elegant first drafts. All right, one of them does, but we don't like her very much.

Yes, this is slow and inefficient. It doesn't matter *how* you get there, but you'll only succeed by finding *your* writing process. I've found that most people work in a way that feels profoundly inefficient: scribbling in different places, transcribing, highlighting, consolidating, and sifting. It feels chaotic, but it's the only way they can get to the final draft. This is a very physical approach, and that's fine. Often people ask me "What writing approach *should* I use?" My answer, much to their annoyance, is "The one that's right for you."

The fundamental point is that you shouldn't be trying to write and edit at the same time — they should be different stages of the cycle. Here's why ...

Writing on the Right Side of the Brain

Now I'm going to — perhaps inadvisably — dabble in some neuroscience again. While this might not be scientifically accurate, it's a practical model for improving writing productivity. You've probably heard the idea that the two sides of our brain are responsible for different activities. The left side is concerned with anything analytical, logical, or linear; the right side, meanwhile, is creative — making imaginative leaps, using intuition, and spotting connections. If we're seeking to create something new, we need to harness the right side of the brain. It's impossible to move logically through something that doesn't yet exist.

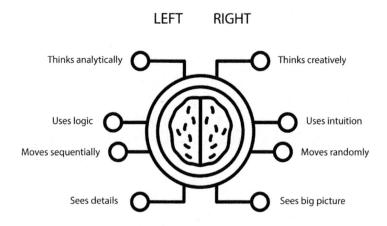

However, the two sides of our brain are often in conflict. The right side spends five minutes cranking out a dozen words, then the left side devotes the next hour to deciding whether they're the *correct* dozen words. You're switching between writing and editing, getting tired in the process, and not making much progress. The trick is to keep writing and editing separate. Our desire to leapfrog straight to the third draft is often about impatience. Instead, think about the craft and the process.

Find an approach that works for you. But, whatever you do, break it down. Writing *then* editing. This is tough to do. It takes practice. You won't ever lose the urge to edit, but you can learn to resist it. If you've ever tried meditation, you'll know how hard it is to let go of thoughts about mundane matters when you're supposed to be focusing on your breath. With practice, though, you'll let go much quicker.

Here are some tips to make it easier:

Switch off your spellchecker — those wiggly red lines are very insistent and distracting.

Write longhand — on the computer, it's too easy to delete and rewrite endlessly (as I've just done with this sentence).

Schedule separate sessions for writing and editing — start treating them as completely separate activities. Sitting in different locations might help, too.

If you're in the early stages of the writing and revision cycle, preparation is vital. Creating the right conditions for writing ensures you'll spend your time productively and avoid rabbit holes.

Avoiding Internet Rabbit Holes

Has this happened to you? You write for five minutes, then realise you need to add a citation. Oh drat, you don't have the details. You'll just quickly look it up online. You find the journal article. Ah, the author mentions a couple of articles you haven't seen yet. You'll just download those, *then* you'll get back to writing. Hang on, this is an unfamiliar term. You'll just find out the meaning, *then* you'll get back to writing. Hmm, it would be irresponsible for you to use this term unless you establish its precise etymology and trace the origins back to Aristotle. Two hours later, you've had a lovely time in Ancient Greece, but still have only 20 words to show for your morning's labours.

The solution is to thoroughly prepare for every writing session by organising citations, reference materials, and our workspace. You're equipping your writing fortress.

Citations

Given the number of citations we need to include in academic writing, looking them up as we go along is a reliable way of losing momentum. Here are three ways to avoid this situation:

1. Use a bibliographic referencing tool such as Zotero

You might already use an alternative such as Mendeley, End-Note, or BibTex. If you're yet to pick one, Zotero is the easiest, and it's free. Make sure you've saved everything to your Zotero (or equivalent) library in advance, then it'll take just seconds to insert a perfectly formatted citation. For more information, take a look at the Resources section.

2. Devise a system of placeholders (e.g. author, date, page)

If you're not ready to use a dedicated tool, you could instead use placeholders. Unless you're working with a huge collection of literature or complex archival records, noting down the author, date and page number should be enough for you to identify the source afterwards.

3. Keep citations in a separate file so you quickly can copy and paste

Maybe you're not using Zotero, but you have your citations in a spreadsheet or Word document. Keep this open on your computer so you can quickly copy and paste them into your writing.

Whatever approach you use, you're aiming to add those references as quickly as possible without resorting to the internet.

Reference Material

When we hit a knotty part of our writing, the tendency is to go back over the reference material. We look to this for comfort and to feel as though we're doing something. *I'll just re-read this article to help get me going again.* The problem is that our head then gets filled with too much information, and we find it impossible to start writing again. It's the same with data and notes.

Make sure, then, that you only have the material you

need for this *specific piece of writing*. For example, if you're writing about a particular quote from a journal article, just have that quote open — not the entire article. If you're analysing one interview, don't have all the others open.

Workspace

We want to reduce the clutter in our minds, but also in our physical environment. If you can *see* lots of unrelated stuff in your writing fortress, it could be distracting you while you're trying to focus. Unpaid bills, shopping lists, half-read books — they'll all be vying for your attention. You want to be wearing blinkers so you can see only what you're working on right now.

What could you do to optimise your workspace? Perhaps you don't have a dedicated writing area, but could you at least clear the table temporarily? Even quickly shoving everything in a cardboard box is a good temporary solution. We're looking to hide potential distractions and stay in the writing zone.

....

ACTIVITY

....

Imagine the ideal writing space. What can you see? What would it look like? What would it contain? If you're imagining an Eames recliner and an amanuensis, that might not be possible. However, perhaps you could recreate at least *some* of those features. If you write in the corner of the living room, could you section it off in some way with a screen or curtain? Could you get a small unit for storing your research materials?

What do you need for your next writing session? Be very specific about the resources, references, and equipment. What *don't* you need? What's just going to distract you? Earlier, we talked about the idea of creating a writing fortress for keeping other people at bay. You also need fortifications against internal distractions — your writing fortress is mental as well as physical.

The Importance of Deep Work

At the risk of losing you to the internet, I recommend you watch Cal Newport's TED Talk on the topic of deep work. He also wrote a book called *Deep Work*, but I'm guessing you don't need anything else to read at the moment. Essentially, Newport argues the importance of completing immersing yourself in a single task and eliminating all distractions. Sounds simple? Try it for ten minutes and see what happens. Your laptop demands updates, there's a Facebook notification requiring your attention, somebody stops by for a chat. It's very unusual for us to enter a state of deep work.

It's not just the distraction itself that causes a problem. Newport explains the concept of *attention residue*. When you switch from one task to another, your attention doesn't immediately follow. Some of your brain cells are still working on that original task, such as mentally composing a response to an email you've just read. Although you're now looking at your thesis again, it doesn't have your full attention.

Perhaps you've taken a quick peek at Twitter and even published a tweet. That only took a few seconds, right? But now your mind is whirring … did anyone like my tweet? Do I have any replies? Has anybody posted a photo of a skateboarding owl? This approach is what Newport calls *shallow work*. It's cognitively undemanding and provides plenty of immediate gratification. With deep work, the payoff is much bigger, but you have to wait a long time. It's human nature to seek an easy win, that dopamine hit of social approval or the satisfaction of having responded to an email.

This state of semi-distraction is seriously affecting our ability to complete demanding tasks. How can you examine a complex question from all angles if your brain is also composing replies and imagining online interactions? Two hours of deep work is worth a whole day of multitasking. We often tell ourselves that we need a vast and clear schedule to get any writing done. What we actually need is frequent and relatively short sessions of deep work. How we organise them depends on lifestyle.

Creating Time for Deep Work

As you can see, creating these slots might involve rethinking your location and habits. In *Deep Work*, Cal Newport describes four different approaches to consider.

Monastic — as the name suggests, this involves behaving like a monk in a monastery. You cut yourself off from other people so you can focus without any fear of interruption. This could be impossible to achieve if you have family responsibilities or lack a room of your own.

Bimodal — this means alternating between a monastic life and your usual mode of living. So, you might take yourself off to a quiet place for an hour a day or a whole day each week. That alternative location is associated only with writing, making it easier for you to slip into work mode. You probably don't have a cabin in the woods, but you might have found somewhere else that's conducive to writing, such as a café or library.

Rhythmic — this is the reality for most people. It's about fixing a time for deep work every day, such as 5-7am, and then protecting that slot vigorously. This is the approach famously adopted by the Victorian novelist Anthony Trollope. He'd be at his desk by 5 each morning and write for two hours before heading off to a day job with the Post Office. He routinely wrote 2,000 words at each sitting. If he finished one novel halfway through his writing sprint, he'd simply start the next one. I should add that as a middle-class man, Trollope benefited from the ministrations of a stay-at-home wife and several servants. I bet we could all get a lot more done if we had domestic staff.

Journalistic — some of us have unpredictable or flexible schedules, so a regular slot won't make sense. The *journalistic* approach is adopting the principle of deep work whenever there's a big deadline. You find whatever gaps are available in your schedule and throw yourself into it. This is better suited to anyone who's self-employed or has a job that involves a lot of travel. If this is you, it's important to be extra vigilant about using those quieter periods.

I used a combination of these four approaches during my PhD. Once a year, I'd take myself off to a residential library in North Wales. I had my own desk where I could completely immerse myself in writing. The internet connection was terrible, so I'd only go online to check something important — aimless browsing wasn't enjoyable. Three times a day, I could wander into the dining room where the friendly staff would sustain me with tasty morsels. I didn't have to think of anything apart from my writing. I would make far more progress during these five days than five months spent at home. Having that time to completely focus was vital for achieving insights and making connections. Of course, I was fortunate in being able to afford this trip.

Is there somewhere you could go?

» Some retreats offer bursaries or significantly reduced fees for students.

» A house swap so you can get away from the usual distractions.

» A cheap hotel or holiday let for a couple of nights.

The only downside of finding a quiet space for ourselves is that there's nobody else to blame if we don't actually write anything. Let's get focused.

Identifying and Minimising Distractions

Some days everything will go swimmingly, others it'll feel like climbing Mont Blanc in flipflops. It's important to establish what's happening on those bad days. Often, it's down to distractions. What's stopping you working? You might want to try this distraction log during your next writing session. You can note down the time of the distraction, where you were when it happened, what you were working on, the type of distraction, and the cause. Was it an internal distraction — something in your head — or someone else being a nuisance?

Once you've logged everything, you can think about ways of eliminating those distractions. Could the solution be to move to a different location? Do you need to shut the door? Get some noise-cancelling headphones, for instance? In *Hyperfocus*, Chris Bailey encourages us to distinguish between fun and annoying distractions. If a distraction is fun, we're much more tolerant of it and therefore more susceptible to its temptations. We also need to identify whether a distraction is within our control. If our work environment is noisy, it might be possible to close a door or window; it's much harder to silence chatty co-workers.

. . . .

ACTIVITY

. . . .

Keep a distraction log for the next week then review it. You can download a template from www.howtofinishyourphd. com.

» What could you do to minimise *internal* distractions? These could include sneaking onto social media, disrupting someone else, or generally finding work displacement activities. Could you use any tools to make it easier for yourself?

» Are there any external distractions over which you *do* have control?

» If there are distractions where you have no control, is there anything else you could do?

Are there any adjustments you can make before your next writing session?

» Different location?

» Headphones?

» Bag of toffees for a talkative colleague?

Often, the source of the distraction is the same technology we're using to write.

Practising Digital Minimalism

At a writing retreat I ran a few years ago, one student was the envy of the group. She apparently had an admirable work ethic, sitting for eight hours at her desk every single day without fail. Yet, when I spoke to her, I heard a very different story. She spent the entire time browsing the internet, especially the *Daily Mail* site. Not only was she horrendously behind on her thesis, but she was also putrefying her soul with reactionary clickbait.

When I first started running workshops for researchers, everyone was clamouring to discover more about technology and how it could make their lives easier. Nowadays, it's a different story. Many of my students want to know how they can avoid social media and actually get some work done. After 30 years of the World Wide Web, most of us have the attention span of a flea and require constant stimulation. This has been compounded by the fact that we now carry tiny computers around with us in our pockets.

In short, smartphones are a menace. And I don't think that's putting it too strongly. Social media is specifically designed to keep us clicking like eejits, terrified of missing out on the next big story about Britney Spears.[8] Seriously, though, technology is no less addictive than narcotics, nicotine, or alcohol, and needs to be treated accordingly. Admittedly, the effects might not be as damaging, but they could seriously harm your doctoral ambitions.

I'm not a misery guts who wants you to bin your electronic devices and do everything the hard way. Quite the opposite. I'm really quite geeky. Sometimes technology *is* the solution, but often it is actually the problem. Cal Newport, who we met earlier, followed up *Deep Work* with a book called *Digital Minimalism*. Here he argues that we need to

....

8 I don't pay much attention to what's happened since 1901, so this is my best attempt at a cultural reference.

develop a personal policy on technology use, otherwise it'll take over our lives. If we don't control social media, it'll control us. Our need for intermittent positive reinforcement and social approval is destroying our ability to achieve more fulfilling goals.

Newport recommends a digital declutter. Here's how it works:

1. Schedule a 30-day period where you'll take a complete break from *optional* technology. It's unlikely you can avoid technology altogether, especially if you're doing paid work. But there are probably some changes you can make, e.g. deleting apps, avoiding social media and aimless browsing.

2. Use those 30 days to explore or rediscover meaningful activities. You might think you don't have time to stop and chat with colleagues, but could you use the 30 minutes you spend on Facebook to build more satisfying connections? Pursuing a creative hobby can help, too. Learning in other areas makes your mind sharper generally.

3. After 30 days, start gradually reintroducing technology into your life. How does it feel now? Is it adding anything? Or is it just a distraction? Newport says FOMO should stand for *freedom* of missing out.

Be honest with yourself. Is that app really boosting your productivity, or is it merely distracting you? Some technology tries to solve the very problem it creates — this sounds laudable but remains a cynical ploy to keep us hooked. Where possible, come up with analogue solutions. If you keep look-ing up spellings online and getting sucked into an internet vortex, buy yourself a decent dictionary and keep it on your desk. You won't then accidentally end up buying a pair of trousers or watching cats shrieking at cucumbers on You-Tube.

If the problem is your desktop, rather than your phone, there are some excellent solutions. RescueTime tracks how long you're spending on the internet and allows you to set goals. For example, you might want to restrict emailing to 1 hour per day, permit yourself just 30 minutes on Facebook, or block all online activity in the mornings. It'll expose all your bad habits, too. I discovered I was checking the BBC news website every 15 minutes, as though there was likely to be some international catastrophe that required my personal intervention (there never was).

For other suggestions, please visit the website www.howtofinishyourphd.com.

In some cases, tomatoes are the answer.

Introducing the Pomodoro Technique

It's no exaggeration to claim that my PhD was utterly trans-formed by the Pomodoro Technique. I still use it most weeks and talk about it almost daily. If you're not familiar with it, prepare for a potentially life-changing experience. *Pomo-doro* is Italian for tomato, and it refers to those novelty toma-to-shaped kitchen timers. Here's what you do:

1. Choose a task to be accomplished.

2. Set your timer for 25 minutes (it doesn't have to resemble a tomato).

3. Work on your task without any interruptions — so, don't check email, make a cup of tea, or talk to the cat. If anything unrelated pops into your head (which it will), quickly make a note of it and return to your task.

4. When the buzzer or bell sounds, take a 5-minute break and record your progress.

5. Repeat, taking a longer break for every 4 tomatoes completed.

The Pomodoro Technique was devised by Francesco Cirillo back in the 1980s. The science behind it is that most of us can focus for only 25 minutes before our mind starts to wander. That's when we resort to faffing and cease making any actual progress. A 5-minute break allows our brain to relax, but it's not long enough for us to lose momentum or forget what we were working on.

You can use those breaks any way you please. Personally, I find it almost impossible to restrict myself to 5 minutes of internet browsing and nearly always overshoot. Also, my mind is then distracted by what I've just been reading, and my thoughts become disordered. I use those breaks to stretch or get a cup of tea. Those of us with dodgy backs can benefit enormously from being told to get up every so often. It's much harder to finish your thesis with sciatica.

For suggestions on Pomodoro timers, see www.howtofin-ishyourphd.com.

The Seven Habits of Highly Effective Tomatoes

Everyone is different, so you'll need to experiment to establish an approach that suits you. Some find 25 minutes too long or require ten minutes between tomatoes; others need a giant 60-minute tomato to make any progress. You might not even find it helpful at all. Some types of work suit this format better than others.

The Pomodoro Technique is highly effective for most of us because it encourages short bursts of focused activity and allows us to break our work down into more manageable tasks. It might take you a little while to get used to it, but soon you'll start thinking of tomatoes as a unit of labour, "Hmm, that looks like a three-tomato task."

You'll be surprised by what you can achieve in 25 minutes, too. It depends on the type of writing (e.g. descriptive, analytical, contextual), but 500 words are feasible if you know what you're going to write. Complete a tomato each day and guess how much you'll have accumulated by the end of the month? 10,000 words. That could be a draft thesis chapter.

If you're struggling to fit everything in your schedule at the moment, just make a commitment to yourself to complete one tomato a day. If that's impossible, you'll need to consider some drastic changes (see Chapter 5). Once you've squashed a tomato for five days in a row, see whether you can squeeze in *two* per day. The key is to not overstretch yourself by setting an unrealistic target. It's much easier to take a short walk every day than it is to run a marathon once a week. Think small and consistent, not big and sporadic.

Once you reach the stage of not noticing the timer, this might mean you don't actually need it. The real strength of the Pomodoro Technique is in helping you get started when resistance is high — "I'll just do one tomato today." Sometimes we need to doggedly pursue one tomato at a time; other days one is enough to find that motivation.

A few years ago, I regularly saw a student who was struggling to finish his thesis. He'd got stuck on the penultimate chapter and couldn't imagine ever finishing. One day, I spotted his smiling face on campus. "Catherine, I've done it!" he shouted. I said, "Well done, that's wonderful news. How did you get through that final chapter?" His response? "It was 150 tomatoes."

My Pomodoro Plan

I worked out that I needed to achieve 20 tomatoes each weekend to maintain respectable progress on my thesis. I gave myself the freedom to divide this up in any way I wanted, but typically it fell into this schedule:

» Saturday morning ~ 10.00-12.30 — 5 tomatoes.

» Relaxing lunch / chores / recreational reading.

» Saturday afternoon ~ 15.30-18.00 - 5 tomatoes.

» Large G&T, stodgy dinner, *Strictly Come Dancing*.

» And repeat on Sunday.

This routine emerged after a period of experimentation. Initially, I'd hoped to get all of my tomatoes out of the way in the morning. Actually, it proved good for me to have a long break in the middle of the day, as this allowed time for ideas to percolate in readiness for the next session. In the final six months, I was also knocking off 2-4 tomatoes each morning before starting my paid work. There was no way I could trust myself to do it in the evening. Yes, it felt relentless, and there was never a day when I didn't have to push myself to do it. However, it gave me a sense of *control* and *progress* — that's wonderfully motivating.

Finding Your Own Approach

Once you've tried the Pomodoro Technique, reflect on these points:

» How long did it take to settle into your writing? This is the period of resistance. Being aware of it helps you realise that it passes.

» Did you get fidgety before the 25 minutes had elapsed? — perhaps you need a shorter session, or to build up to 25 minutes.

» Was it frustrating to stop after 25 minutes? — either a longer session might be better, or maybe you don't need the Pomodoro Technique at this stage. You can always deploy it another time when it's harder.

» Did you have trouble regaining focus after the 5-minute break? — were you getting engrossed in something online? If so, try a physical activity that doesn't require too much cognitive effort.

» On average, how much did you achieve during a tomato? — once you understand your process, it becomes easier to decide how many sessions you'll need over a week. It's helpful to consider the *type* of writing, too. For example, "I can produce 500 descriptive words or 100 analytical words."

Sometimes a tomato isn't enough. We need to create accountability.

Creating Accountability

> "All of human unhappiness comes from one
> single thing: not knowing how to remain at rest
> in a room." Blaise Pascal

One of the biggest challenges with academic writing isn't necessarily the writing itself, it's actually keeping ourselves in the chair. As soon as we hit a rocky part, there's an overwhelming urge to wander off and tackle an easier task — even when we're mid-tomato. We tell ourselves, "This is far too difficult *today*. I'll come back tomorrow, and it'll definitely be easier." Unless we push through those tricky parts, though, it's impossible to make significant progress. The solution is to either get some velcro pants or to create *accountability*.

Some universities offer Shut up and Write sessions where students get together physically or virtually to support each other. If this isn't available at your institution, you can check the website (www.shutupwrite.com) for events open to everyone. You could also agree with a few friends or colleagues to write at the same time each week. Either send each other messages at the start and finish of each session or use Zoom to stay connected throughout.

Another alternative is Focusmate (www.focusmate.com). This online tool matches you with a stranger so you can watch each other write. Yes, it does sound a bit creepy, but it's incredibly effective. You choose a 50-minute slot through the online calendar, then click on the link to connect with your partner. You have a brief chat at the beginning to introduce yourself and explain what you're going to work on. Then you get writing. At the end, you have another brief chat to share what you've achieved.

Whatever approach you use, you need *accountability*. When you make a commitment to another person, you're more likely to turn up. If you just make a commitment to yourself, there's a tendency to let something else take priority. The presence of another person ensures we stay in our chairs and keep going, even when it's a struggle. Of course, your partner won't know if you're faffing about on Twitter, but you'd probably look a bit shifty during the final chat.

If you're struggling to commit to accountability sessions, you might be suffering from procrastination.

Overcoming Procrastination

In *The War of Art*, author and screenwriter Stephen Pressfield describes the daily battle to overcome resistance. Even though we know we *should* be writing and serving our best interests, there's a powerful pull in the other direction. We feed resistance with our fear, that fear of getting started. As Pressfield writes, "Master that fear and we conquer Resistance."

If you're experiencing that overwhelming feeling of resistance, spend some time considering *why*. Once you've identified the problem, you can find a solution. Are you finding it ...

Dull? Pick a bit that interests or excites you and start there. There's no need to start at the beginning and slog through. Indeed, it's often easy to write the introduction once you've got everything else in place. Starting with that lively paragraph might be enough to recover your motivation.

Frustrating? What's missing? Perhaps you don't have the right piece of data or an appropriate quote. This doesn't happen often, but occasionally we're trying to write too soon.

Hard? Are you giving yourself a mammoth task? Does your to-do list say "Draft Chapter 3"? If so, break it down into more manageable chunks and just focus on one at a time.

Chaotic? It's time to return to the planning stage. A few years ago, I was writing a chapter for an edited collection. Nothing seemed to fit together, and I was stuck in an endless loop. Eventually, I took a step back and mind mapped my concept. I realised that I was actually writing *two different* chapters. They were in conflict with each other and pulling me in different directions.

Futile? Start with why. Remember those reasons for doing your PhD? Take a look at them again.

Another technique for overcoming procrastination is to *write* about it.

Getting Going with Freewriting

Freewriting is a useful tool in any writer's toolkit. The idea is that you write continuously — no stopping to edit or think — just keep going. This writing isn't destined for your thesis, it's just to get you going. Some potential uses are:

» To warm-up.

» To clear your head.

» To motivate yourself.

Five minutes of frantic typing might be enough to achieve your momentum. Possible prompts include:

» What excites me about this piece of writing?

» How will I feel when it's finished?

» Why have I been struggling with it?

I often use the prompt "What am I really annoyed about?" That shifts those distracting thoughts from my head and on to the screen. I'm then in the right mindset for some academic writing.

You might use some more specific prompts to work through crunchier problems:

» My thinking has changed because …

» One of the challenges I'm facing is …

» Something I need to address is …

Removing the need to sound 'academic' can help you to write more freely.

ACTIVITY

Make a list of 20 potential writing prompts. It doesn't matter if some of them are nonsense — the more you create, the better chance you'll have of creating a few winners. Keep them as a note on your computer or a page on your desk so you can quickly refer to them if you get stuck. You'll undoubtedly come up with other ideas to add later, too.

As we'll see in the next chapter, these prompts can become an essential part of your writing routine.

Conclusion

Showing up at our desk each day isn't enough — we have to be *intentional* about how we use that time. Unless we're vigilant, other people can invade our writing space. Even worse, we can fall victim to self-sabotage. Identify those blocks of time for deep work and decide how you're going to protect them. Who or what is threatening your writing fortress? How can you pull up the drawbridge? Can you fire some rubber arrows at repeat offenders from your turret?

According to Gloria Mark's paper 'The Cost of Interrupted Work: More Speed and Stress', it takes an average of 23 minutes and 15 seconds to return fully to a task once we've distracted ourselves. So, a whole tomato is lost each time you check email or flick through Twitter. You're still making progress in this less-than-focused time, but you'd be far more productive and insightful if you weren't distracted. Jumping between tasks might *feel* as though you're on top of everything, but really it's just avoiding the important stuff. If you've set aside a block of time for deep work, *that's* your priority. Don't let anything else claim precedence.

Only by reducing the constant flow of information and stimulation can we focus on our own thoughts and make real progress. Procrastination is the enemy of productivity, and they're engaged in an ongoing war. We have to fight that battle every day, which means developing effective strategies and processes that work every time. Predictable effort means predictable results means predictable progress.

....
ACTION POINTS
....

»   Think of some PhD-related activities you could pursue in odd moments.

»   Imagine your ideal writing space. Which elements are you able to recreate in reality?

» If you're struggling with focus, keep a distraction log for a week.

» Create 20 freewriting prompts to help you get going.

....
SUMMARY
....

» Create the right conditions for writing, both physical and mental.

» Don't write and edit at the same time.

» Prepare everything in advance for your writing session so you don't need to go online.

» Identify distractions and minimise them.

» Take a moment to understand *why* you're procrastinating and find a different approach.

....
TROUBLESHOOTING
....

I can't find any time or space for deep work

Firstly, revisit the Eisenhower Matrix in Chapter 5. Is there anything you could drop at least temporarily to make time for writing? Don't think of it as a permanent change for now — you're just experimenting. Once you've successfully scheduled a couple of deep work sessions and made progress, you'll feel motivated to find time for some more. If you're struggling with a distracting environment, try 5 minutes' free-writing to identify potential solutions. Ask yourself "Where could I write?" and see what comes out. You might surprise yourself.

I can't stop editing when I'm writing

This is hard. I once coached an engineer who was finding it impossible to switch off the left side of his brain. He was so used to thinking logically and sequentially that creating more than a few words an hour felt like a Herculean task. He decided to spend an entire day on the right side of his brain to see what happened. Every time his logical mind fired up, he quickly shut it down and carried on creating. Admittedly, he looked utterly exhausted by 5pm, but he'd written *thousands of words*.

I'm still in the grip of procrastination and can't find a way out

It takes time to change our habits, especially when they've been embedded over many years. Your brain may have been hijacked by a monkey. You'll meet this entertaining but unhelpful sidekick in the next chapter. In the meantime, just focus on what you're doing *right now*. You can't control whether you'll procrastinate tomorrow or the next day, but you can change what you're doing in the present moment.

7. Building Routines and Keeping Going

> "We are what we repeatedly do. Excellence, then,
> is not an act, but a habit." Aristotle

When we have a productive day, we feel on top of the world. At last, I've managed to overcome procrastination, defeat my inner critic, and avoid distractions. However, it takes more than one successful session to finish a thesis. Equally, we don't shift a few pounds by avoiding biscuits for one day or get fit by making a single trip to the gym. We need to make *consistent* progress to reach that goal. This is not to say that we have to become machines, rather that we need to *mostly* do the right things repeatedly.

Perversely, we can also become *too* productive. While this can work in the short term, eventually we crash and burn and become incapable of doing anything. As we saw in Chapter 5, that's the Fantasy Zone. Just as we set limits on the thesis at the beginning of this book, we also need to set some limits on ourselves. In the middle ground, we somehow muddle through and make some progress. But we don't understand *why* it's working. Without taking the time to reflect on our processes, we can't fine-tune our performance by doing more of the good stuff and ditching the unhelpful habits.

In this chapter, we'll develop some processes and tactics to ensure you make consistent progress. We're looking for predictable results. If I follow *this* set of steps … *that* will be the outcome. While this sounds straightforward, many factors can stymie us. Our emotions take over, and we tell ourselves stories — "I'll just spend today watching Netflix, then I'll definitely start my writing routine *tomorrow*." Or "I'll work really late this evening, but will get an early night *tomorrow*." The problem is that tomorrow doesn't exist. The compounding effect of these bad habits builds up to a major problem.

Now we're going to devise some writing routines, create good habits, and measure progress. This way, you'll get the compounding benefits of *good* habits. We'll also confront perfectionism and what to do on days when our brain refuses to cooperate.

Understanding the Chimp Paradox

Although writing a PhD is supposed to be a solo effort, we all have a collaborator. Unfortunately, not an especially helpful one. Have you ever sat down to write and then been seized by an overwhelming urge to buy socks online? That's your monkey. The Chimp Paradox is a mind management model developed by Professor Steve Peters. Under this model, the mind is separated into three teams, each with its own agenda and way of working:

The Human (that's you) is located mainly in the frontal lobe. It's associated with logical thinking and likes facts.

The Chimp mostly occupies the limbic systems and prefers feelings, emotions, and impressions. Our chimp is a permanent sidekick.

The Computer, spread throughout the brain, is where we store programmed thoughts and behaviours. Both the Human and the Chimp have admin rights to the computer.

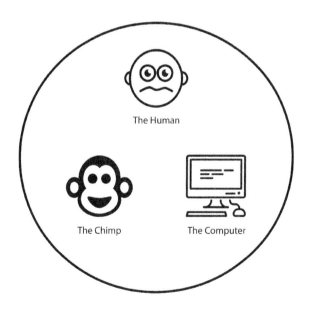

The Human and the Chimp can act independently, in cahoots, or against each other. The Chimp *paradox* is that this monkey sidekick can be either our best friend or our worst enemy. If you repeatedly sabotage your efforts and act impulsively, it means the Chimp has the upper hand. The challenge is to store information in the Computer to help us manage the Chimp.

Here are some tips on keeping your Chimp under control:

Give it some bananas. Chimps like rewards and respond well to praise. Our Chimp is more likely to let us get on with our work if there's an incentive. This might be a sticky bun, a night out, or just a relaxing evening. If you promise your Chimp a reward and don't follow through, it'll be hell-bent on thwarting you tomorrow.

Show it some evidence of progress. Giving yourself a big tick each day for hitting a writing target delivers a banana-like emotional high. You could even award yourself gold stars on a chart. We're conditioned from an early age to crave this type of recognition, and I'm not sure it ever really goes away. A few years ago, I gave all the attendees of a writing retreat a cheap plastic medal. They were thrilled. You deserve a medal — this is hard.

Take your Chimp for a walk. Simians need exercise, otherwise they get fractious. We can't ignore our emotions altogether; instead, it's a case of venting them safely. This means finding the right situation and the right person. If you're feeling rubbish about everything, is there somebody you can trust to let you vent without fear of judgement? If not, you could try freewriting for five minutes. There's plenty of evidence to show that writing about our feelings has an immediate therapeutic effect. Once it's out of our heads, we can return to the task in hand. For persistent negative thoughts, take another look at the ABCDE worksheet in Chapter 2 to develop a system for overcoming them. Remember, the thoughts never go away completely, we just get better at dealing with them.

Distract your Chimp. Sometimes we indulge the Chimp because it's easier than getting on with our work. After all, chimps are fun. We can learn to recognise when this is happening and take steps to avoid it. For example, ignoring social media when we're writing is a good way to keep the Chimp quiet. Otherwise, it's not long before we're caught in a spiral of righteous anger and impotent despair.

OK Computer

The Computer part of your brain is where you store the *processes* that govern the Chimp. Once you recognise the tactics your Chimp uses, you can program *scripts* to ensure that you, the Human, remains firmly in charge. Scripts are essentially routines or algorithms — a series of tasks we follow without thinking. A routine can make us feel like automatons with no free will. But if we don't give ourselves instructions, we're putting our Chimp in charge. A reliable process is the best way of ensuring we get our most important work done. Let's create some routines.

Devising a Startup Routine

It took me a long time to realise that I couldn't simply sit at my desk and expect academic writing to emerge from my head. I'd sit there frowning at the screen and wonder why nothing was happening. After ten frustrating minutes, I'd decide to check my email or look at Twitter, as if that was going to help me get into the zone.

Just as we wouldn't expect to compete in the 110m hurdles without warming up, it's the same with writing. We need to ease ourselves into it gradually. This way, we can almost sneak up on ourselves and start writing academically before our brains have realised what's happening. We can do this by creating a startup routine or algorithm.

The advantage of effectively programming ourselves is that it doesn't leave any room for judgement. Ask yourself, "Should I do some writing this morning?" and your brain will frantically come up with at least a dozen reasons why it can't possibly happen now. Instead, follow a clear set of instructions that have already been set out.

The steps of your startup routine will depend very much on your personal preferences, but here's what it might include:

Make a cup of tea, or beverage of your choice — some people like to use a special writing mug. This mug is *only* used when writing, so it signals to the brain that they're moving into this mode.

Get comfortable — if you're not sitting comfortably, you're likely to develop aches and pains. Once this happens, you associate writing with physical pain and your body (as well as your mind) will recoil from it. Spend a few moments adjusting your workspace. Perhaps you can optimise your chair or get a cushion.

Switch off the internet — as we've established, the internet is a giant conspiracy to prevent you from getting any work done. Make sure you've downloaded everything you need in advance so you don't disappear down any rabbit holes.

Do 5 minutes' freewriting — this gets you warmed up, clears your head, and helps get those synapses firing. You're writing without putting any pressure on yourself to produce anything sensible.

Tackle an 'easy' tomato — when I say 'easy', it could also be 'exciting' or a least marginally more attractive than all the other tomatoes. The aim is to give yourself a quick win that gets you motivated.

Now you're flying.

Pulling the Trigger

In *Atomic Habits*, James Clear explains that the successful creation of habits involves establishing triggers. What's the event that precedes the desired activity? Rather than wondering when we're going to write, we know we've just had lunch, so now it's time to go and do a tomato.

In the final year of my PhD, I had to fit in a writing session before starting my paid work. This was tough. The only way this happened was if everything ran like clockwork:

» [Trigger] Alarm goes off at 6am

» Roll out of bed

» Put on pyjamas

» Make a cup of tea … then into my startup routine.

If anything got in the way of this routine, it broke the script.

....

ACTIVITY

....

Have a think about a potential startup routine. It might take you a little while to get it right. Give it a try, adjust, and try again. This is all about removing the friction between you and your writing. Break down each step as much as possible — you want a series of micro-steps, each of which is easy to accomplish and leads naturally to the next.

Try your routine for 5 days and reflect on progress. Is this working?

Sometimes, these startup routines can be *too* effective. Yes, really. We find it impossible to stop and are still hammering away 8 hours later. Although this might sound like a nice problem to have, it's not a long-term strategy — you'll soon be exhausted. You also need a *shutdown* routine.

Adding a Shutdown Routine

You might think that writing too much is a nice problem to have. Over time, though, it can cause problems. Without an exit strategy, we're tempted to keep writing until exhaustion sets in, or our mind is buzzing with distracting thoughts when we're trying to switch off. A shutdown routine helps you ease out of writing mode and also prepare for your next session. Again, the exact steps depend on your personal preference, but here's what it might include:

Use bullet points to quickly jot down any ideas — this gets them out of your head and removes the fear of forgetting them. You'll also have a clear structure for tomorrow.

Make a quick note of what you want to do tomorrow — e.g. I want to finish the introduction to Chapter 2, then check the references. Again, you won't need to spend time tomorrow trying to remember what you'd intended to do.

Do 5 minutes' freewriting — this helps you reflect on your session and come out of academic mode. You might create some additional prompts, such as "What went well today?" or "Is there anything I could try tomorrow to make my writing session more productive?"

Update your progress chart — this gives you visible evidence of progress, and it's very satisfying. I'll share an example in a moment.

Tidy your workspace — clearing the clutter might make your desk seem more inviting tomorrow. If your desk also happens to be a dining table or in your bedroom, it also means you're not distracted by the sight of your writing materials when you want to relax.

If you've ever watched Velodrome cycling on the telly, after the race, the competitors clamber on a static bike and keep pedalling. This is because their legs are still moving at a frenetic pace and need to gradually slow down rather than just stopping suddenly. The shutdown routine has a similar effect on your mind. You can't be having all those clever thoughts and suddenly switch them off. Capture, reflect, prepare, then relax.

ACTIVITY

Come up with your own shutdown routine. You might want to add a reward at the end — something entirely unrelated to your PhD and preferably in a different environment. Watching YouTube videos on your laptop doesn't shift you completely into a different mindset if you've been sitting in front of it all day. Creating those mental and physical boundaries allows your brain to recover.

Becoming a Creature of Habit

Apparently, it takes 66 days to establish a habit. A *good* habit, that is. I find it takes a matter of hours to get into a *bad* habit, such as rewarding myself with cake for mastering a slippery paragraph. If something becomes part of your daily routine, it starts to feel odd if you *don't* do it.

I tried a 66-Day Challenge a few years ago. I was procrastinating about writing a book chapter and kept telling myself that I simply didn't have time. Meanwhile, I was also complaining that Facebook was making me miserable and sapping my emotional bandwidth. Rough calculations showed I was spending around 25 minutes each day on Facebook — one tomato, in our new currency. Instead of exposing myself to compulsive oversharing and attention-seeking, I resolved to spend 25 minutes writing after dinner each evening.

Dinner became the trigger. I'd finished eating, so the next step was to arise and perch at my desk. I'd set my timer, then start typing. Sometimes it was painful, occasionally it was unproductive, but often I'd squeeze out a few hundred words. Once or twice, I even enjoyed myself. By the end of the challenge, I had created 17,500 words — in just 25 minutes a day, time I would otherwise have wasted on creating data for Mark Zuckerberg to sell.

I also made two useful insights:

» Firstly, I'd always told myself I couldn't write in the evenings. Although it's unlikely I'd have been able to sustain a longer session, this short stint was enough to make progress.

» Secondly, around halfway through the 66-Day Challenge, I felt automatically pulled towards my desk in the evenings. I didn't necessarily *want* to write, but it felt weird and uncomfortable if I didn't.

I kept a chart on my door and put an X in the box every time I completed my writing challenge. My Chimp was delighted with this evidence of progress and egged me on every day.

You shouldn't be working on your PhD every day, but there's no reason why you couldn't *write* every day. It doesn't have to be about your research. Maintaining a simple journal keeps you in touch with your thoughts and feelings and flexes your writing muscles. The more writing you do, the more natural it feels. If 66 days seems too long, you can download a 30-Day Challenge chart from www.howtofinishyourphd.com.

Once you've established the habit, you'll also need a way of tracking progress on your thesis.

Measuring Progress

"You can't manage what you can't measure."
Peter Drucker

It's hard to get an objective sense of our progress. When we ask ourselves, "How do I *feel* about my PhD?", the answer is usually, "Dreadful! It's all nonsense and everyone else is doing much better than me." Emotions are a terrible judge of what's really going on. What we need, then, is *evidence*. As I mentioned in Chapter 2, we need a way of reminding ourselves that those feelings aren't true. If you were incapable of writing, you wouldn't have been accepted onto a PhD programme.

A writing audit is a good way of engaging the neocortex and bypassing that unhelpful limbic system. This template helps you move through the different drafts and sections of your thesis and also shows you exactly where you are. You might notice that the stages in this example correspond to the Writing and Revision Cycle (see Chapter 6). At a glance, you can see what you've done and what's left to do.

Make your own, or download a copy from www.howtofinishyourphd.com. Create a more detailed version of the audit that includes all the sections of your thesis. Try to break it down into small chunks, so you're able to tick off at least one of them each session. You need that sense of achievement.

You can either keep it on your computer and update it, or print a copy to stick on the wall. At the end of each session, update your word count and tick the boxes to show what you've completed. It's a Word document, so you can quickly adapt it to suit your own thesis structure and stages. You can also think about a word target for those sections. You might only need 2,000 words for your methodology, but unless you've given this some thought, you could accidentally end up with five times as much — that's a lot of wasted effort that could be deployed elsewhere.

Tracking your word count makes sense when you're in the intensive writing phase. It's immensely satisfying to see yourself edging towards the target. At later stages of the Writing and Revision Cycle, it's no longer meaningful. Indeed, you might be deleting words. You'll need a better measure. Perhaps you're now aiming to reduce the word count? Track this instead. Note where you are now and what you're aiming for.

We'll be looking at editing techniques in the next chapter. Once you have a strategy that works for you, you can build it into this audit template.

....

ACTIVITY

....

» Download the writing audit template and adjust for your own thesis.

» Work out what you need to measure.

» Link it with your plan to make sure you keep moving. If you're using sprints, map the stages of the audit to those chunks.

Including Review Points

If you stop making progress at any stage, it's time to sit back and review the situation. It's impossible to make a plan that works magically in all circumstances — our current self is trying to imagine how our future self will perform and what will be happening around us.

Schedule some time each week to consider how it's going. Ideally, do this in the form of a journal by asking yourself some questions:

» How much did I achieve this week?

» Was it in line with what I hoped?

» If yes, what made it a productive week?

» Could I recreate these conditions?

» If no, what went wrong?

» Were there problems I could've anticipated and prevented?

» What could I do differently next week? New location? Different time of day?

And look at where you are on your overall plan. Roughly on target? Sailing ahead? Or languishing behind? If you're struggling, you can consider:

» What's slowing me down?

» Am I striving for perfection?

» Or trying to do too much?

» Is my timescale simply not realistic?

» Is there anything else I can stop doing to make more time for my thesis? At least temporarily.

Do some calculations, too. How many useful words can you write in half an hour? How many do you need? Of course, this is a rough calculation, but it gives you an idea. It stops you from pretending you can produce submission-ready prose in a day. Once you know that your personal best is 500 words a day, it's hopeless to routinely aim for 1,000. This helps you come up with a more realistic plan.

Avoiding Perfectionism

Usually, we grind to a halt because we're trying to get something perfect. "I need to get Chapter 1 polished before I can progress to Chapter 2." Two years later, you're still wrestling with Chapter 1, and you have three months left to finish the rest of your thesis.

The Pareto Principle describes the idea of *uneven distribution*, that roughly 80% of the effects come from only 20% of causes. It was developed by Italian polymath Vilfred Pareto, who discovered that around 20% of the peapods in his garden contained 80% of the peas. Then he calculated that 80% of the land in Italy was owned by 20% of the population, and it spiralled from there.

Although this isn't an exact formula, you might well find that most of your writing emerges from 20% of your time. That remaining 80% is spent trying to get everything exactly right — making endless revisions and worrying whether it's good enough. Rather than maintaining a strong momentum, we slow right down, and progress becomes imperceptible.

We can use this 80/20 rule to set some limits. Aim to get your thesis chapter 80% complete, then submit it to your supervisor. Their input will make it much easier for you to fix that final 20%. Thinking back to the Writing and Revision Cycle, you're just making sure than everything makes sense so someone else can follow your argument and provide constructive feedback.

Progress, not perfection. Or use my mantra: "lower your standards and keep going".

Dealing with Darwin Days

In 1861, Charles Darwin wrote in a letter: "But I am very poorly today and very stupid and hate everybody and everything." Ever had a Darwin Day? Yep, me too. It's frustrating when we've put aside some time for deep work, then our brain refuses to cooperate. There are a few options to consider, though:

1) Do you need a rest? If our bodies and brains go completely floppy, perhaps they're trying to tell us something. Taking a day off allows us to recover and then attack our thesis with renewed vigour. Obviously, it becomes problematic if we designate every day a Darwin Day. We need to stay in tune with ourselves and learn to recognise whether this is exhaustion or just procrastination. You can only tune in once you've slowed down.

2) Could you work through some of those easier tasks that we identified in Chapter 6? Although they're not desperately exciting, these jobs get you closer to the finish line without requiring too much brainpower. This is precisely the stuff you don't want to be bothered with when you're in flow, so they're best saved for low-powered sessions.

3) If you're lacking in motivation, is there a trigger that would get you back in the mood? Amitoze, a PhD student in AI, told me that he watches videos on machine learning to rekindle his enthusiasm. This gives him some context for his writing and inspires him to get going. Other students teach themselves a new skill, do some exploratory reading, or try writing more creatively.

....

ACTIVITY

....

Create a list of activities for Darwin Days. What could you still achieve, even when everything feels rubbish?

Ideas include:

» Tidying formatting.

» Downloading articles.

» Checking regulations (dull, but vital).

» Organising your workspace.

» Verifying citations.

No single approach will work every time a Darwin Day strikes. The longer the list, the better your chance of finding a suitable activity. If you work through all of them and still nothing's happening, it's a good idea to give yourself a day off. That could be a sign that you're overdoing it.

Conclusion

Focusing on processes might seem boring, dangerously close to a routine. Surely as creative people, we should wait to be seized by an exciting idea? Paradoxically, imposing a routine gives us *freedom*. This intentionality means we can get the most important stuff done in the shortest possible time. Then we've got much more time for other activities. Constraints can be liberating.

Relying on willpower is exhausting; following a routine is simple. Yes, it feels as though we've lost our power to decide, but *not* having a routine doesn't get results. You need to reach the point where it's easier to work than not to work. This means developing a process, removing friction, and making work the default option. If you're slightly off target for one week, that won't be too bad. Remain off-target for a few months, though, and you're in serious trouble.

Make sure you have a realistic idea of what's happening so you can adjust. Introducing review points ensures you're not just working hard, you're also working *effectively*. If ever you get stuck, consider whether you're pursuing perfection instead of progress. Set yourself *realistic* targets and establish the best way of pursuing them. A PhD doesn't need to be an exercise in masochism.

....
ACTION POINTS
....

» Devise startup and shutdown routines.

» Download the writing audit and adjust it for your own purposes.

» Create a list of activities for Darwin Days, when everything feels rubbish.

. . . .

SUMMARY

. . . .

» When it comes to your writing routine, make sure it's the Computer and not the Chimp who's in charge.

» What you measure, you manage.

» Track your progress for a sense of achievement — only trust the evidence, never your emotions

» Small and consistent beats big and sporadic.

» If you're tired, either take a break or pick an easy task.

. . . .

TROUBLESHOOTING

. . . .

I'm unable to stick to my routine

Are you trying too hard to achieve the perfect process? No system on earth makes everything completely effortless. Aim for a process that gets you started. You can always refine it afterwards. Make sure it's realistic — are you pushing yourself too hard? Start small and build up, e.g. one tomato a day. Once you can achieve that comfortably, you can accommodate additional tomatoes. Or perhaps you've lost sight of your priorities?

It could also be that you're bored. Many PhD students drop out in the final year when they've almost finished, just because this last stage can be so dull. You've made all the exciting discoveries and insights, now you spend day after day trying to pull it all together. There's no other way around it. Add a five-minute freewriting session at the beginning of your writing routine and use it to remind yourself *why* you're doing this.

My monkey is running riot

You need to spend some time on monkey management. Just like that critical voice, it never completely goes away — you just learn to deal with it. And that means getting to know your monkey and its ways. Maybe at the moment it wants bananas, but next week it could be something else. One student came up with a name for his monkey (Tarzan) so he could acknowledge his presence and address him directly. The good thing about doing a PhD is that nobody is in the least bit surprised if you start talking to an imaginary monkey.

Remember — although the Chimp loves quick hits, like watching YouTube videos, it also loves recognition. Make sure you're acknowledging successes. Use the 30-Day Challenge worksheet or agree with a friend to keep each other up-to-date with progress. Don't forget to give yourself rewards, too.

I've got a brilliant idea that I need to pursue before I finish my thesis

All new ideas feel more exciting than our current project. This is because it's a loosely-formed thought and we're entirely oblivious to how much work is involved in getting off the ground. Believe me, starting a business or writing a novel is *not* easier than finishing your PhD. By all means, keep a note of your idea. It'll be waiting for you when you've submitted your thesis.

8. Getting Ready for Submission

"To write is human, to edit is divine." Stephen King

One of the magical moments in a PhD occurs when you find yourself clasping a full draft of your thesis. It's still messy, but everything is there — although not necessarily in the right order. Even if you started out with a strong structure, you probably went off at tangents, introduced some random thoughts, or entirely forgot what you were supposed to be saying. With some revising and polishing, though, you can reimpose some order and coherence.

When I say *polishing*, I don't mean a quick buff. Here we're talking about *French* polishing. If you're unfamiliar with French polishing, it's a painstaking process that involves applying many thin coats of shellac to wood. Although laborious, this technique reveals the texture of the wood and produces a lustrous finish. This is what you want for your thesis — for that texture to be visible to your examiners.

Editing tends to be the activity that gets squeezed at the end of the thesis. You're up against that tight deadline and keep thinking of extra stuff you need to add. Even if you've already checked those chapters a few times, by making these last-minute changes, you inadvertently introduce new errors and inconsistencies. This makes it much harder for your examiners to follow.

Performing a thorough edit is lengthy and repetitive, but in this chapter, we'll break it down to make it more manageable. I can't pretend it'll be fun, but it should be effective. I'll get you to think about what your examiners are seeking, then guide you through a three-stage process to ensure you've covered everything systematically. Then you'll be ready for the next magical moment: submission.

Why is Editing Important?

In case you're thinking about submitting that baggy draft and hoping for the best, here's why editing is essential.

Creates a good first impression — when the examiners open your thesis for the first time, they'll immediately notice your writing style. This initial impression provides examiners with cues about other aspects of your work. If you haven't taken the time to edit your writing, does that mean you've adopted a similar approach to your research methods or your analysis? Creating a bad first impression means you'll be playing catchup throughout the rest of the thesis.

Ensures clarity and eliminates ambiguity — you've no

doubt read articles where you're not entirely sure what the author means. You *think* you've grasped it, but the writing is ambiguous. There could be a missing word, a double negative, or perhaps a term that has several potential meanings. Although your examiners will probably work it out, you want them to spend their time absorbing your arguments rather than struggling to understand them. If they're confused, this might result in an unnecessarily combative viva.

Makes your readers happy — the first paragraph gives them a sense of whether this will be a pleasurable experience or a slog. They're no different from us. We all have that sinking feeling when an author's writing style makes reading feel like a chore. Here's the voice of experience, Sue Johnston:

> [E]xaminers approach the task of reading a thesis with needs very similar to readers of any new piece of work. Enthusiasm to be engaged with new ideas in their field quickly dissipates if confronted with work which is not 'reader-friendly'.[9]

This isn't to say that your thesis needs to be perfect. As we've established, it's not a book (yet). The emphasis here is on clarity and precision. You're not trying to be Hilary Mantel.

Some examiners will reject theses with more than a certain number of errors. They'll insist that the candidate edits it properly before resubmitting. This is embarrassing and also holds up the examination process. You must schedule enough time

....
9 Johnston, S. (1997) 'Examining the examiners: an analysis of examiners' reports on doctoral theses', *Studies in Higher Education*, 22(3): 333–47.

to produce your thesis to the required standard. In this chapter, I'll guide you through a systematic approach so you can get your thesis ready for submission. We'll start with structure, then flow, and finally the smaller details. If you think back to the Writing and Revision Cycle from Chapter 6, you don't want to spend time editing something you'll later delete. While you're editing, you need to think about your reader. In this case, that reader is an examiner.

Thinking About Your Examiners

Those of you only part-way through your PhD might not want to think about your examiners at this stage. But they are the readers of your thesis. You are writing for *them*. It perhaps feels as though you're writing for your supervisor, but he or she won't be examining your thesis. It's worth considering these possibly unidentified people to understand what they're seeking in a doctoral thesis. You might think those examiners are only interested in cutting-edge research and won't care about how it's presented. That's definitely not true. If you don't believe me, take a look at this quote:

> There is sometimes an assumption that the examiner is an expert in the field and does not have the expectations of a 'normal' reader. It is worth remembering that all readers require assistance to understand the work, that they feel distracted and irritated by poorly presented work, and that they appreciate well-written, interesting and logically presented arguments.[10]

10 Johnston, S. (1997) 'Examining the examiners: an analysis of examiners' reports on doctoral theses', *Studies in Higher Education*, 22(3): 333–47.

Indeed, a few examiners have told me informally that it doesn't matter if the thesis is earth-shattering, the candidate will still end up with major corrections if they haven't taken the trouble to present it properly. Nobody enjoys indigestible prose. As the novelist Shirley Jackson once said, "a confused reader is an antagonised reader". You don't want an antagonised examiner.

What are your examiners looking for?

Originality — as you'll already know, one of the key criteria on which your thesis will be judged is originality. Examiners want stimulation, rather than a rehash or synthesis of what they already know.

Significance — it has to be significant, too. They must see evidence that this project is justified and actually contributing something meaningful to your field. Your thesis might be both original and significant without that being evident to your examiner. If you bury your insights beneath too much waffle and contextual material, your examiners won't spot it.

Rigour — your thesis is an opportunity to demonstrate research skills. Examiners rapidly lose confidence in work that's sloppily presented and riddled with errors.

Coherence — as mentioned above, they want to follow your argument without getting in a tangle.

Context — the only way you can make a claim to originality and significance is by showing an understanding of your field.

This might be by identifying gaps through your literature review and clearly showing how your work fits.

How is a thesis examined?

A survey of doctoral examiners[11] concluded that there are three main ways in which they approach a thesis:

1. They get a general overview by reading the abstract, introduction, conclusion, and table of contents. Then they read from cover to cover.

2. They skim through the entire thesis. Then read more slowly from cover to cover.

3. They read once from cover to cover very slowly and thoroughly.

Method 1

This is the most popular approach. As you've hopefully noticed, this means your introduction and conclusion are crucial. Your examiner is reaching their initial judgement based on those elements. It's essential, then, that your main arguments, claim to originality, and findings are expressed unambiguously. Make sure, too, that your table of contents provides valuable metadata in the form of section headings that give a sense of your argument and flow.

....
11 Mullins, Gerry, and Margaret Kiley, '"It's a PhD, Not a Nobel Prize": How Experienced Examiners Assess Research Theses', *Studies in Higher Education*, 27.4 (2002), 369–86.

Method 2

If you're a skim reader yourself, you'll know that this method benefits from keywords and concrete terms applied consistently. Waffly paragraphs might be skimmed over altogether. More about concrete terms in a moment.

Method 3

Examiners who employ the final method are the most dangerous. They'll take meticulous notes throughout and spot any inconsistencies or discrepancies. As they're reading through only once, you have just one opportunity to get those ideas across. The examiner will probably refer to their notes before your viva, rather than returning to your thesis, so you're relying on them having grasped all the detail.

Of course, not all examiners will follow these methods, and you can't predict what approach they'll take. Anecdotally, though, it's a reasonable assumption that they'll read your introduction and conclusion twice, and everything else once. So make sure your thesis is bookended with what you want them to take away.

....

ACTIVITY

....

Consider the different ways in which examiners might approach your thesis. How does this affect your presentation? What needs to appear in your introduction and conclusion? Could you optimise the structure?

Breaking Down the Editing Process

As we've established, you're writing a thesis for your examiners. These people are the gatekeepers to your PhD. It's all about convincing them that you've achieved the required standard. It's imperative, then, to provide them with a carefully curated showcase of your skills. You need to get them from A to B via the most direct route, with no confusing detours, digressions, or deadends. This means looking at your thesis from *their* point of view.

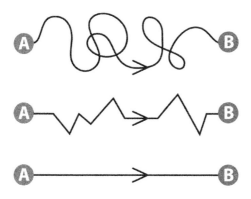

You might by now have a full draft of your thesis. If so, well done. It probably resembles a baggy monster, with random parts and a few unattractive features. After all, the creative process can be messy. Now, though, we're going to use the left side of your brain to think more logically, critically, and analytically about your writing. Before you jump in, let's break down the editing process into five stages. This approach will save you time and also make it easier. The stages

I recommend are:

1. **Structure** – getting the main elements in the right place.

2. **Flow** – arranging your paragraphs in a logical order.

3. **Signposting** - providing a roadmap for your examiner.

4. **Clarity** – ensuring consistency and eliminating ambiguity.

5. **Details** - making tiny tweaks through proofreading.

I'll explain them all in more detail in a moment. The important point is that you need to complete the top-level editing before you tinker around with the details. Otherwise, you're just creating more work for yourself. And don't attempt multiple levels at once — your brain can only handle so much. First, we look at structure.

Stage 1: Establishing Your Structure

Once you have a full draft of your thesis, it's much easier to work out your story. You might not think of it as a story, but there is almost certainly an underlying narrative. This is what guides your reader from the introduction to the conclusion. Editing the structure is all about revealing this narrative arc and removing anything that isn't part of the story.

By this stage, of course, your thesis is quite unwieldy. It's not much fun scrolling back and forth through an enormous Word document. I'd suggest that you map it out instead.

Here's what you'll need:

» An empty wall or other blank space.

» Some oblong sticky notes.

» Lots of square sticky notes.

» Marker pen.

Write each of your chapter titles, not the numbers (they might be working titles at this stage) on the oblong sticky notes and position them in a line at the top of your space. Now use the smaller sticky notes for jotting down the elements of each chapter – this might be sub-sections, themes, key ideas – and arrange them vertically under each chapter heading. You're not going into too much detail right now – this is to give you an overview. Aim for a maximum of ten sticky notes per column.

Eventually, you'll have a map of your thesis. Now you can scan through and see what's happening. Here are some points to consider:

» Are the chapters proceeding in a logical sequence? If you need to reorder them, write the numbers on some extra sticky notes and position them above the chapter titles.

» Do any of the chapter elements belong elsewhere? Flag them on your plan.

» Can you spot any duplications across chapters? Make a note to either delete the duplicated content or remind yourself to add a signpost or link (e.g. "As I discuss in chapter 2…").

» Have you spotted any gaps that need to be filled, such as some context to link two sections?

» Is there anything that doesn't fit? Are there diversions or digressions that might confuse the reader? Mark those with a red X.

I appreciate that it's tough to delete chunks that represent hours of work down the research mines, but a tighter thesis helps to make your argument clearer. Those deletions aren't lost, either. You can turn them into journal articles, blog posts, or add them to a future book.

Hopefully, you now have your structure sorted. Using

your map, you can reorganise your chapters and remove anything superfluous. Restructuring can be a challenging activity, but it'll result in a stronger thesis and one that's easier for you to defend.

Here are some points to remember:

» Arrange material to suit your narrative, not the order in which you wrote it.

» Remove anything superfluous.

» Eliminate duplications.

» Keep your research questions and aims in front of you to avoid deviations

» Don't get distracted by small details at this stage – you're just looking at the overall structure.

» Take a backup before making any changes to your thesis.

Stage 2: Improving Flow

If you imagine your thesis as a house, the previous step was all about getting the foundations right. Now we're going to think about the bricks or building blocks. You probably have a lot of these building blocks, but they're not necessarily in the right order. We'll achieve a logical flow by rearranging them. Importantly, we're ignoring the smaller details for now. You don't arrange the cushions until you've built your walls.

First of all, a few thoughts on paragraphs. Usually, a paragraph shouldn't really be shorter than three lines. A paragraph is a building block that's making an important point in your piece of writing, so it needs to be reasonably substantial. In novels, there might be a very short paragraph for dramatic effect, but there's not really a good argument for doing that in a piece of academic writing. Also, a paragraph shouldn't contain more than one key idea. Otherwise, you can overwhelm your reader who's trying to follow that argument.

Each paragraph break allows your reader to have a short pause before they move onto the next idea. And there should be a structure and a purpose to each paragraph. Sometimes when we're writing, we get carried away and just add in random paragraphs that aren't really contributing a great deal. Now's the time to ditch those. Each paragraph should be connected to the previous paragraph. There's a clear sequence for your reader over which your argument builds.

Reverse Outlining

Let me introduce you to a technique called *reverse outlining*. This, I reckon, is the best way to improve the flow of your argument and produce a coherent thesis. Here's what you do:

Step One

> » Print a draft of your completed chapter.

> » Number the paragraphs in the margin.

» For each paragraph, write a concise bullet point summary (it should fit on one line and describe the purpose of that paragraph).

You now have a list, which is easier to work with than an entire chapter.

Step Two

Now scan through your bullet list and remain alert for the following:

» Are your paragraphs following a logical sequence?

» Are there any duplications?

» Gaps where you need to add a segue?

» Giant leaps that require additional context?

» Digressions that might confuse the reader?

» Any paragraphs that are doing too much work and should be divided?

» Or some that are lacking a specific point and can be ditched?

It'll take you a few hours to reverse-outline a 10,000-word draft, but it's time well spent. We all repeat ourselves, go off on tangents, and repeat ourselves. Edit the bullet point list, then use it as a model to work through your draft.

Top Tip

Make sure you *cut* and paste paragraphs when you're moving them, rather than copying – otherwise you can end up with duplicates. If you don't trust Word not to lose your text, change the font colour of the paragraph you've just copied to red, then you'll notice it later. It's also still there in case the clipboard loses the text. As before, take a backup before making changes.

Optional Step Three

It's common for us to rely too much on secondary sources and using quotations from more established academics to make an argument. Consequently, our own voice gets lost, and the thesis becomes a synthesis. To ensure your voice is apparent, you need to remove some of that scaffolding.

Using your reverse outline bullet point list, devise a colour-coded scheme to flag the different types of writing in your draft. For example:

RED = secondary sources

AMBER = context

GREEN = original argument/findings/conclusions, etc.

There's no right balance between secondary sources, context, and originality, so spend some time thinking what might be appropriate for your project. Perhaps you could prune a quotation from six lines down to one and leave some room for your own observations.

Remember:

» Each sentence and paragraph should propel your reader from the introduction to the conclusion.

» Be prepared to delete anything that doesn't fit the narrative.

» A logical flow helps your reader understand the argument.

» Your argument must be evident throughout.

» Don't worry about smaller details at this stage – you're purely getting your paragraphs in the right order.

Stage 3: Adding Signposts

Once you've got your structure in place and those paragraphs in the right order, you can start adding some signposts. Signposts help your reader navigate around this very long piece of writing — they need a sense of where they've been, where they are, and where they're going next. Signposts might include descriptive headings, cross-references, and emphasis of argument. They're not very exciting to write, but they can make a big difference to the reader's experience. I'll wheel in Professor Johnston again to illustrate my point:

> [Examiners] appreciate work which is logically presented, focused, succinct, summarised and in which signposts are used to help readers understand the path they are taking through the work.[12]

Think again about your examiners. They're probably reading your thesis alongside a dozen journal articles, a few book chapters, and hundreds of student essays. It's unlikely they'll have time to read your work in long sessions and might therefore be dipping in and out over a few weeks or even a couple of months. Consequently, they need reminders about what you've already covered and clear summaries of your arguments. Once they reach chapter 4, they won't remember something you mentioned in chapter 1 — that might have happened several weeks ago.

Here are some examples of signposts:

Chapter or section outlines

At the beginning of every chapter or section, you should explain how it's structured. This isn't spoiling the fun, it's helping your examiner understand what's coming. They can then focus on the arguments.

....
12 Johnston, S. (1997) 'Examining the examiners: an analysis of examiners' reports on doctoral theses', *Studies in Higher Education*, 22(3): 333–47.

Mini-conclusions

This means summarising your arguments as you go. Although you'll have explained your claim in some detail, following it up with a succinct summary helps the examiner follow your overall argument. You can think of this as a sub-total. Remember, your examiner shouldn't be struggling to fathom your argument or its significance.

Emphasis of argument

Similarly, you might want to remind your examiner of related arguments. For example, "As I argued in Chapter Two, this text ….".

Cross-references

If you've explained a theory or concept earlier on, for example, in your literature review, you don't want to repeat it later on. However, you still need your examiner to know that you've talked about it. In this case, you can simply say something like, "Here I apply the theory of X, which I discuss more fully on p3." "In this section, I draw on the theory of X, which I introduce on p3 of my literature review." You don't want your examiner thinking, "Why hasn't this candidate explained her use of this theory?" You have! It's just elsewhere.

Headings, sub-headings, beginnings of paragraphs

Headings and sub-headings break up the text, giving the examiner natural pauses, and also signal what's to come. Your examiner might only read your thesis cover-to-cover once, then go back and skim through to remind themselves of your arguments. In this case, those headings provide an essential roadmap. If your headings just say 1.1, 1.2, it'll be easy for them to get lost.

As Pat Thomson points out on her excellent blog,[13] signposts provide a roadmap not only for the reader but also for you. While we're writing a very long document, it's easy to get lost ourselves. When it comes to editing a full draft of your thesis, you'll be grateful to your former self for making everything clearer.

ACTIVITY

Once you've reached the signposting stage, you can use the checklist below. *Have you ...*

» Provided an outline of your structure in the introduction and at the beginning of any sub-sections?

» Summarised your argument at the end of each section?

» Emphasised your argument?

» Added cross-references?

» Used descriptive headings and sub-headings?

13 www.patthomson.net

Stage 4: Boosting Clarity

We're now going to zoom into the actual words and sentences. I hope you resisted fiddling with them during the earlier stages, as that usually just results in duplication of effort. You've got the structure, flow and signposting in place, this is the moment for consistency and clarity.

Sentences

Sometimes bad things happen to good sentences. We know what we mean, it all sounded good in our head, but then an absolute horror emerges on the page. I mentioned earlier the importance of introducing pauses between paragraph for your reader. You also need pauses *within* sentences. If you think of a musical score, the composer adds pauses or rests through notation and also varies the tempo. It would be quite dull if the whole piece moved at a consistent pace. It's the same with writing. We need to give the reader a rest and not make the tempo too predictable.

One of the easiest ways to make our writing clearer is to write shorter sentences. It's always tempting to squeeze as many ideas as possible into one triumphant sentence — "There's this, and there's that, and oh yes, here's another thing!" This is exhausting for your reader, as they'll probably have to re-read it several times. Even if you like writing mammoth sentences, I'm willing to bet you don't enjoy *reading* them.

Here's an example:

> Twentieth-century diary fiction draws on the developments of diary writing and fiction from the letter-journal novel of the eighteenth century to the *journaux intimes* of the Fin de Siècle, and in the early twentieth century the diary novel began to reflect similar interests in interiority and psychology, depicting themes such as doubt, fear, introspection and passivity, as diaries began to be seen as a source of world-weary ennui and malaise, as a pernicious and damaging habit.

Any idea what that means? No, me neither.

Unless unavoidable, sentences shouldn't be longer than three lines. Any longer and the human brain struggles to process all that information. When you spot a long sentence, read it aloud. If you turn blue halfway through, it's definitely too long. If you can't say it, you shouldn't write it either.

Varying the length is good for your reader, too. If you do need to have a long sentence, then follow it up with a much shorter sentence. You could also use semi-colons, colons, parentheses or dashes to break up that loooooong sentence. These punctuation marks allow your reader to pause, reflect, and absorb. Here's an example of a long sentence, but it's been broken up using a semi-colon and dashes, so it's straightforward to read:

> Britain's discovery of abundant coal seams and invention of technologies able to convert this fuel into mechanical power played a crucial role in the Industrial Revolution; but there were other funda-

mental drivers of change – political, economic, geographical and social – which historians have only just begun to explore, and others that continue to be overlooked.[14]

I'm not going to bang on about punctuation now, but I will recommend the *Penguin Guide to Punctuation*, which is very short and lively and packed with great examples.

A Few Words on Words

> "When I use a word," Humpty Dumpty said
> in rather a scornful tone, "it means just what I
> choose it to mean - neither more nor less." Lewis
> Carroll, *Through the Looking Glass*

The English language is very complicated even if, like me, you've spoken it for nearly half a century. Unless we check our work systematically, it's easier to introduce ambiguities, inconsistencies, and waffle. These six techniques[15] will tighten up your prose:

1. Use power verbs

Routinely, we resort to relatively weak verbs, like have, make, do, and show. If we replace those with more specific verbs, it makes our writing stronger and more precise. For example, *establish* is much stronger than show. This first example is fine, but it's a little bit vague and weak:

....

14 Almeroth-Williams, Tom, *City of Beasts* (Manchester: Manchester University Press, 2019), p.14.
15 Some of these techniques are adapted from Helen Sword's excellent book *Stylish Academic Writing*.

"In what is known as the Golden Age of detective fiction, the majority of writers were women."

If we use instead the verb *dominated*, this is suddenly much stronger:

"Women writers dominated the Golden Age of detective fiction."

It's also a lot more concise. You can see there are far fewer words in the second sentence, but it says exactly the same as the first sentence. Before getting carried away with power verbs, make sure you understand the conventions in your discipline. In some areas, you're expected to be more tentative and use verbs like *suggest* rather than *demonstrate*. Take a look at some theses and speak to colleagues to find out how much latitude you have.

2. Avoid zombie nouns

If you haven't come across these zombies before, they're *nominalisations*. The more memorable name was created by Helen Sword.[16] These are nouns that have been formed from verbs, adjectives, or other nouns. Essentially, they're words we invent to make it sound more academic. These words are very abstract, so it's harder for the brain to process them. And if we get a lot of these abstract words in one sentence, we can reach overload. Like zombies, these nominalisations suck the life force out of our writing. Here's an example:

....
16 For an entertaining explanation, watch Helen Sword's TED-Ed Talk – https://youtu.be/dNlkHtMgcPQ.

> The development of the category of middlebrow fiction during the interwar period intended to effect the containment and delineation of the type of mass-market literary fiction which had aspirations to the status of high culture. Middlebrow literature had strong associations with the middle class and its increased power and with innovations in the mechanisms of literary circulation such as libraries and book clubs. Factors which made a significant contribution to the definition of middlebrow fiction, in accordance with the assertions of the critics of the interwar period, included its tendency to lack seriousness and authenticity, its use of content and form which was taken as evidence of failure to challenge the reader, its tendency towards soothingness and palliation, and, most significantly, the class position of its readership and authorship.

You can see there are lots of words such as *containment*, *delineation*, and *contribution*. And then some wholly invented terms like *soothingness*. This is all quite jarring for the brain. There aren't that many clear concrete terms that we can understand and hold onto. Anyone who's skim-reading will struggle to get a sense of your argument. Here's the same paragraph again, with lots of those nominalizations removed:

> During the interwar period, the category of middlebrow fiction was developed to contain and delineate the type of mass-market literary fiction that aspired to the status of high culture. It was strongly associated with the increasingly powerful middle class, and the new mechanisms of literary circulation such as libraries and book clubs. Factors which made a significant contribution to the definition of middlebrow fiction, in accordance with the assertions of the critics of the interwar period, included its ten-

dency to lack seriousness and authenticity; its use of content and form which was taken as evidence of failure to challenge the reader; and its tendency towards soothingness and palliation. The most significant defining factor was the class position of its readership and authorship.

You can see here the language is much more vivid and concrete. It's easier to read and, again, it's much shorter, too.

3. Clarify ambiguous words

Most of us find we've got loads of examples of *this* and *it* littered throughout our writing. We know what we mean by *this* or *it*, but our reader won't necessarily. In the example below, you can see that *this* could either refer to the idea of work becoming bound up or it might relate to the idea of the emphasis. We could go back and reread the previous sentence to work out what is meant by *this*. But that's extra work for the reader, and you're slowing them down.

> For middle-class young women, work had now become bound up with notions of patriotic duty and self-improvement, even though there was still considerable emphasis placed on the central importance of women's domestic role. **This** had changed social attitudes to the idea of women's paid work outside the home.

You could say 'This emphasis' rather than just 'this'. Yes, that's repetitive, but that's better than being ambiguous.

4. Eliminate unnecessary words

If you bury your arguments under lots of extra words, it's much harder for you reader to follow them. Examples abound in academic writing, such as "on a regular basis" rather than just "regularly", or "an increased appetite was manifested by all the rats," instead of simply "all the rats ate more". There's no extra information conveyed in the more cumbersome version. Look out for these habits in your own writing. Often, we're up against the word limit anyway, so going through and eliminating these unnecessary words can help enormously.

5. Keep related words together

When you have a related noun and verb, make sure there's not a huge clause in between them. Otherwise, your reader is likely to forget the noun was at the beginning of the sentence. They have to go back and reread it. In this example, the noun is *writers* and the verb is *set*. There should be more than about 10 words in between. Or perhaps you could use parentheses if you do have to include an extra piece of information in between.

> Many novice **writers** at the beginning of their academic careers, hopeful of the production of elegant and impactful academic prose and delusional about the amount of work achievable in any given amount of time, **set** themselves excessively ambitious targets.

6. Use words consistently

As you're reading through, make a mental or physical note of the terms you're using. Have you applied them consistently? For example, do you in some places refer to Great Britain, and the United Kingdom in others? Also, check your tenses. Are you veering between past and present? There's no right answer to the tense you should deploy, but they might relate to the stage of your thesis. For example, in the Introduction, "I will argue that…"; in the main body "I argue that…"; in the conclusion, "I have argued that…". It's up to you, but be consistent.

ACTIVITY

Take a section of your thesis, around 2,000 words, and work through this checklist. Have you noticed any common problems? If so, make a list so you can look out for them elsewhere.

- » Use power verbs

- » Avoid zombie nouns

- » Clarify ambiguous words

- » Eliminate unnecessary words

- » Keep related words together

- » Use words consistently

Stage 5: Tweaking the Details

> "My spelling is Wobbly. It's good spelling but it
> Wobbles, and the letters get in the wrong places."
> A. A. Milne, *Winnie the Pooh*

Proofreading is perhaps the one activity I dislike even more than housework. This stage is unbelievably tedious but absolutely crucial. Typos creep in all the time, especially when we're stressed and frantically editing the text. The only way to approach proofreading is calmly and systematically. And you need to do this right at the *end* of the Writing and Revision Cycle. Otherwise, you'll have to go back and recheck all those additions and deletions.

Should you hire a proofreader?

Perhaps you've seen ads or received emails promoting proofreading services at reasonable rates. These companies are generally best avoided. They often subcontract the work to distributed freelancers who are paid low rates and may not be native English speakers. They're relying on the spell-checker in Word — which you could do yourself and then spend the money on treats instead.

It's completely understandable if you want to hire someone. Perhaps you're dyslexic, you've struggled writing in English, or you don't want to look at the wretched thing any more than is absolutely necessary. I get it. In this case, make sure you hire a *professional*. In the UK, I'd suggest approaching the Chartered Institute for Editing and Proofreading.[17] Its members are qualified and experienced, with some having additional training in academic writing. You can probably also find one who understands your subject area. This isn't strictly necessary, mind you, as they're just checking for *tiny details* at this stage.

Throwing money at the problem can be satisfying, but there are a few things to be aware of. Proofreading is expensive. It's a laborious process, and you're paying by the hour. The cost for an 80,000-word thesis is likely to be at least £600. If you go for the cheapest, you'll get someone who is reading less carefully. Having said that, even great proofreaders miss typos. None has a success rate of 100% on a complex document like a thesis, but they're likely to do a better job than you.

Bear in mind, too, that great proofreaders are in demand. You'll need to negotiate a start date with them and make sure they have the final draft ready to start work. They'll have lots of other projects booked in with little flexibility. As you might have guessed, working with a proofreader is likely to mean completing your thesis even earlier. This is another part of your project to manage.

What do proofreaders do?

Unlike editors, proofreaders won't change the sense of your text. They don't generally point out that you've used the wrong word or that you've made a factual error. Their role

....
17 www.ciep.uk.

is to spot spelling mistakes, grammatical solecisms, and keyboard mishaps. This is why they don't need to be an expert in your subject. If there are peculiarities in your field that might confuse them, provide a short briefing document.

Some will also help with formatting, ensuring that headings, figures, and citations are consistent. They'll need a copy of the guidelines for your institution. Naturally, this takes a lot of time, so it'll be factored into the cost. Be clear on your expectations before starting.

Universities sometimes have strict rules around the use of proofreaders and editors. This is to ensure that candidates don't benefit from additional input. Check with whoever is responsible for postgraduate researcher regulations at your institution. There might be an approved list of professionals or guidance on what help you are allowed to solicit.

Before you hire a proofreader:

» Check with your university — is there an approved list or guidance?

» Make sure you're getting a professional — search the database of the Chartered Institute for Editing and Proofreading.

» Clarify what they're going to do — e.g. editing, proofreading, formatting.

» Prepare a briefing document to explain anything that might be confusing.

» Decide how you'd like them to work — e.g. tracked changes in Word.

» Consider deadlines — by what date will you need to get the final draft to them?

» Remember that they probably won't catch everything.

DIY Proofreading

If you want to give it a go yourself, here are some tips:

Print it out: if you're working on the screen, it's far too tempting to make sweeping changes. That's absolutely not what you should be doing at this stage. You know I'm right. Working on paper is less tiring, too. A different font might help you get some perspective on it, too — it then looks less like *your* writing.

Do it in short bursts: your eyes will get tired, and also it's bloody boring. If you're yawning and staring at the same page, you've become ineffective. I recommend using the Pomodoro Technique to keep your eyes and brain sharp.

Read sloooowly: if you're a fast reader like me, this is excruciating. But there's no point in proofreading quickly — you'll just miss half the mistakes and have to start all over again. Boo. You're aiming for no more than 20 pages per hour. I follow each line with a ruler. This prevents me from skipping ahead, and I can use it to hit myself when I keep spotting the same stupid mistake.

Use a screen reader: software that reads your text to you. This makes missing words more conspicuous. Funnily enough, I tried it out on this page and immediately noticed a missing word. When we read silently, our brain often fills in the gaps.

Crowdsource some help: not many people will love you enough to read your *entire* thesis, but you might be able to bribe them to check a section for you. Even better, organise a reciprocal arrangement with another PhD researcher. If you're thinking, "But they might steal my ideas!"[18] No, they won't. They're far too worried about their own thesis.

Using Software

Apart from the fact I hate proofreading, I'm not very good at it either. Consequently, I'm a big fan of Grammarly (www.grammarly.com) a web-based tool and Word plugin that checks your spelling and grammar. I was sceptical at first but heard nothing but praise from students and other writers. The free version offers only a limited number of checks, but the premium product is highly sophisticated. It's not cheap, admittedly, but Grammarly is comprehensive and less costly than an actual proofreader.

....

18 At least one person shouts this out during my editing workshops.

Although Grammarly does a lot of the gruntwork for you, you'll still need to guide it. Some of its grammar quibbles are, I think, overly pedantic and slightly archaic, such as getting excited about split infinitives. You'll need to go through and check everything it's flagged and decide whether you want to accept the recommended change. This could easily take several days on a full thesis. Still, that's faster than doing it yourself manually. The annual subscription is pricey, but you could just pay for one month's access when you reach those very last stages.

You're not going to catch all the errors — I'm not sure that's possible with a thesis — but you want to eliminate as many as possible. A few typos here and there are forgivable, but a thesis littered with errors is unacceptable.

How Much Time Do You Need?

The most common question I'm asked by PhD students is "how long does it take to edit a thesis?" Unsurprisingly, it depends on several factors: length, complexity, your speed, how much other stuff you've got on, and what time is left. Ideally, you should dedicate a 12-week sprint to editing. If you're studying part-time, you might need two sprints, unless you're able to take some time off from your other responsibilities.

Go back to your weekly planner and add in some deep work sessions for editing. Think about how much energy you need for the different editing tasks. Making your formatting consistent is much less demanding than getting a clunky paragraph to make sense. The session length and time of day will depend on the stage:

Structure — it's much better to do this in long stretches so you can hold the entire project (or at least large chunks of it) in your head. If you're doing your PhD part-time, block out a series of weekends for this activity.

Flow — you'll need at least an afternoon to reverse outline a thesis chapter. It's not too mentally demanding, though, as you're just trying to get everything in the right order rather than creating anything new.

Signposting — although this is a relatively straightforward task, again you need to remember what you've said earlier in the thesis. It's best done in longer sessions.

Clarity — tackling those sentences and words is both fiddly and challenging. However, it can be achieved in shorter sessions that you fit around other tasks. If you have lots of non-PhD responsibilities, could you squeeze in a tomato before breakfast or after dinner?

Details — this is another activity that can (and indeed *should* be done in short bursts). You absolutely don't want to spend an entire day proofreading.

One of my students found himself an empty seminar room on campus for sorting out his structure. Using the whiteboards, he mapped out his entire thesis, taking photos of the most effective structures. He then projected the chosen image on the screen. Next, he printed a copy of his thesis, cut it into pieces, and started moving them around. This was literally cutting and pasting. This might sound a bit odd, but physical movement can really help. We get a more spatial sense of our project, and it gets us away from the screen. Often, we're trying to work all this stuff out in our heads, and there simply isn't room.

For many people, this is the worst part of the PhD. Endlessly revising your own work can feel soul-destroying. You're no longer coming up with new ideas, making insights, or identifying connections — it's just the seemingly endlessly drudgery of getting everything in the right place. If you're at that stage, here are a few words just for you:

»   You're nearly there. A year ago, you'd have been delighted to reach this stage.

»   Editing, although laborious, is improving your thesis and your chances of viva success.

»   It *will* come to an end.

You need to be especially gentle to yourself during this phase. Set some clear boundaries between work and rest, devise some treats, and keep reminding yourself how far you've come. This is the point at which many people abandon their PhD. They feel entirely overwhelmed by the colossal task of imposing order on this seemingly loose collection of ideas. Like any complicated project, though, the secret is to break it down and tackle it one chunk at a time.

Knowing When to Stop

Nobody has ever said to me, "Catherine, I've said everything I wanted and my thesis is exactly what I imagined it would be." Don't expect happiness, necessarily, just a sense that you've done what you could. With infinite time and resources, you really could produce a Theory of Everything — but that's not realistic. It's a compromise. There's always a temptation to put it in the bin and start all over again. Please don't.

You just need to produce something good enough for the examination process — something that looks a bit like a thesis. As I've said a few times, this isn't a book, and you're not aiming for perfection. The purpose of the thesis is to convince two or three examiners that you're an independent academic researcher. Although there's no official way of checking that your thesis is 'done', you can use this checklist:

Have you …

» Identified your core argument?

» Stated your argument clearly in the introduction and conclusion?

» Provided evidence to support your argument?

» Explained the significance or implications of your argument?

» Addressed all research questions posed at the beginning?

» Added enough context to explain your argument?

» Arranged the material in a logical sequence?

» Inserted signposts to guide the reader?

» Included all relevant citations?

» Solicited and incorporated feedback?

» Checked and implemented the style guidelines?

» Proofread everything?

You can download a checklist at www.howtofinishyour-phd.com.

If you've checked all the items on the list, then you're probably ready for submission. Naturally, you'll need to discuss this with your supervisor. Should disagreements arise, take a look at Chapter 4. This is not the time for your supervisor to suggest major changes.

Don't be tempted to keep tinkering in the hope of achieving perfection. You and your examiners will have very different ideas of perfection — and it's *their* idea that matters. Rather than trying to anticipate what they're seeking, submit a thesis that meets the requirements outlined above. The examiners will then tell you what you need to do to improve it. You can think of the viva as a live peer review session. If you submitted an article to a journal, you wouldn't expect the editorial board to accept it with no revisions — that's pretty much unheard of. It's the same with a PhD. Although some people do pass without corrections, this is unusual. Accept that you'll need to make some changes.

There are two types of thesis:

» a perfect thesis

» a *finished* thesis

The first one doesn't exist. Don't aim for perfection, else you'll still be plugging away in 10 years' time. You've got other stuff to do. Get it good enough, then submit.

Conclusion

Although editing can be the toughest part of the PhD, it might make the difference between a pass or fail. If your examiners can't work out your argument, how will they grasp its originality or significance? Systematically working your way through the different editing stages produces a thesis that you'll be proud to submit. It'll also be easier to turn it into other publications afterwards.

Few people enjoy editing their own work. Students tell me, though, that having a system to follow makes it much easier. Rather than just attacking that baggy draft in a frenzy, there's a predetermined sequence of steps, each with a clear purpose. With steps in place, you can also track your progress and create milestones. And once you're familiar with various activities, you'll have a better idea of how long everything takes.

And I'd like to leave you with this thought: we'd all like to write elegantly, but it's much more important to achieve clarity. Clarity is vital in academic writing. We're trying to get that complex idea from our head into someone else's. You can pursue elegance afterwards, once you've got your PhD. For now, this is an examination, not a book.

....

ACTION POINTS
....

Consider the different ways in which examiners might approach your thesis. How does this affect your presentation?

Follow the Editing Process:

» Map out your structure with sticky notes.

» Reverse outline your paragraphs.

» Add signposts.

» Check for monster sentences.

» Make your words stronger and less ambiguous.

» Get some feedback.

» Then check those tiny details.

SUMMARY

» Make some time in your project plan for editing, ideally a 12-week sprint.

» Break down your editing into stages and don't attempt more than one stage at a time.

» Be systematic.

» If you're hiring a proofreader, allow extra time.

» Think about your reader always.

» Remember that it's never going to be perfect.

TROUBLESHOOTING

I'm close to submission and worry I don't have enough time to meet examiners' expectations

Do your best. Nearly everyone gets corrections, so try not to think of your thesis as 'finished'. Focus on making your argument clear and compelling, and don't worry about elegance. You never know exactly what the examiners are looking for. You might think it's perfect, but still get asked to make major changes. Look back at the checklist to ensure you've covered the essentials.

I really need help, but I can't afford to hire someone

It might be worth asking at your university to see whether there are any grants available. If not, could you afford the paid version of Grammarly for a month? The built-in grammar and spellchecker in Word is quite good these days and will find most common errors if you use all the features. A final run-through on Grammarly should then reveal any less obvious problems.

Maybe you could also ask a friend or colleague to proofread a short extract of your thesis. They're unlikely to have the time or inclination to go through the entire document, but they might spot repeated errors that you can quickly fix. Don't be tempted to go for a cheap proofreader.

It's all rubbish

Most of us feel this way. Even though it's tempting to abandon the whole sorry mess, it's much better than you think. By the final year of your PhD, it's really hard to get any perspective on your own work. Try to be as systematic as possible and leave it up to your examiners to judge.

Conclusion

"The beginning is always today." Mary Shelley

We've almost reached the end of our PhD adventure together. Perhaps you haven't yet finished your thesis, but I'm hoping you now at least have a strategy for getting there. Importantly, this needs to be *your* strategy — what's worked for someone else won't necessarily be effective for you. Coming up with new ways of working might feel like extra labour when you already have a big project on your hands, but you're developing skills that will help you beyond the PhD, too. Once you've conquered this challenge, you'll be ready for anything. The self-knowledge that results from doing a PhD is just as important as the qualification itself.

As we've seen, you need that sense of purpose — in terms of why you're pursuing a PhD and what's required of you. Then it's a matter of adopting the right mindset and breaking everything down into more manageable chunks. As project manager, you're responsible for every aspect, including managing your team. In addition to maintaining this overview, you'll have to think about what must happen each day so you can stay on track. Remember, you want the compounding effects of *good* habits rather than the disruptive variety. Finally, magically, something emerges that looks a bit like a thesis. Then you can edit it ready for your waiting examiners.

If you're still struggling with motivation, consider the cost of inaction over different timeframes: 1 month, 6 months, 12 months. Perhaps it won't be too bad if nothing changes over the next few weeks — you could always scramble to catch up. But what if you're still in this position next year? What would be the impact emotionally, financially, and physically? Think about what you could do *today* to improve the outcomes for your future self. And don't worry about tomorrow — it doesn't exist.

In case you're a super-efficient reader who's skipped through to the conclusion, here are my three main tips for reaching the finish line:

» Completion is not just about getting things done, you have to get the *right* things done.

» The PhD is an examination, not a book.

» You need to decide what you're *not* doing by setting some limits.

You can't control how clever you are, but you *can* decide how hard you work. And it's not just about working hard, it's working smart. Find a process that works for you, then *trust* that process. Focus on what you do each day, make sure you're heading in the right direction, then you'll have a finished thesis. I can't pretend it'll be easy, but just think how good it'll feel.

Please let me know when you submit — catherine@phdprogress.com. I'll perform a celebratory jig, just for you.

Before You Go

Thanks so much for reading this book — I hope you found it useful. If so, I'd really appreciate a review wherever you bought it.

You'll find lots more support at **www.phdprogress.com**.

Bibliography

Books on Productivity and Focus

David Allen, *Getting Things Done*

Ray Bradbury, *Zen in the Art of Writing*

Chris Bailey, *Hyperfocus*

James Clear, *Atomic Habits*

Dale Carnegie, *How to Stop Worrying and Start Living*

Stephen R. Covey, *The Seven Habits of Highly Effective People*

Carol Dweck, *Mindset*

Anne Lamott, *Bird by Bird*

Brian P. Moran and Michael Lennington, *The 12 Week Year*

Cal Newport, *Deep Work*

Cal Newport, *Digital Minimalism*

Steve Peters, *The Chimp Paradox*

Stephen Pressfield, *The War of Art*

Martin Seligman, *Authentic Happiness*

Martin Seligman, *Learned Optimism*

Books on Academic Writing

Patrick Dunleavy, *Authoring a PhD*

Rowena Murray, *How to Write a Thesis*

Diana Ridley, *The Literature Review*

Helen Sword, *Stylish Academic Writing*

Larry Trask, *The Penguin Guide to Punctuation*

Journal Articles

Johnston, S. 'Examining the Examiners: An Analysis of Examiners' Reports on Doctoral Theses', *Studies in Higher Education*, 22.3 (1997), 333–47.

Mark, Gloria, 'The Cost of Interrupted Work: More Speed and Stress', *CHI '08: Proceedings of the SIGCHI Conference on Human Factors in Computing Systems*, April 2008, 107-110.

Mullins, Gerry, and Margaret Kiley, '"It's a PhD, Not a Nobel Prize": How Experienced Examiners Assess Research Theses', *Studies in Higher Education*, 27.4 (2002), 369–86.

You can find this list with clickable links and some additional suggestions at: www.howtofinishyourphd.com.

Acknowledgements

Although it's my name on the cover, this book wouldn't have been possible without the thousands of PhD students I've encountered over the last 6 years. I can't mention you by name, but please know how much I've enjoyed meeting every one of you. Most of you have now been 'doctored' and won't even see this book. I will single out Viktoria Doppelstein, though. When I threatened to abandon this project partway through, Viktoria's disappointed face inspired me to continue.

I've probably run more than 400 workshops and writing retreats by now. Thank you to all the university staff who helped organise them. Clare Hunt, Steve Colburn, Rob Witts, Laura Chapman, Helen Hampson, Adam Kreimeia, Katy Stoddard, Bethany Logan, Helen Webb, Sophie Valeix, Marine Joly, David Ratcliffe, and Alanna Smith deserve a special mention. The Foundling Museum in London provided a wonderful venue for many sessions, while Connie & Cooper kept us all nourished and happy during numerous Thesis Boot Camps.

Thank you, too, to the PhD community on Focusmate, especially my regulars: Amitoze, Arne, Alan, Puleng, Safi, Nikki, Sinéad, and Natalia. Even though I've finished my PhD, I still need encouragement with other writing projects.

Excruciatingly, I have to repeatedly take my own advice.

Emma Winston created most of the illustrations and provided many insights while working with me on a placement through CHASE DTP.

My own supervisor, Jenny Bourne Taylor, gave me a much-needed fillip during a terrible slump and is now a good friend. I've since published some of Jenny's work, which put me in the odd position of giving my supervisor feedback on her writing.

Clare Griffiths has been a great accountability partner and cheerleader, both for this book and my other pursuits. Although I've never met her, Joanna Penn has provided heaps of practical advice on self-publishing through her podcast The Creative Penn.

Finally, the biggest thank you goes to my partner, Tanya Izzard. Not only did she encourage me throughout my PhD, but she also edited and indexed this book. Neither would have got done without her. We both pursued our PhDs part-time, managed to remain married, and graduated at the same time. When I'd really had enough of my thesis, Tanya reminded me how annoyed I'd be if I had to sit in the audience and look pleased for her. She always knows the right thing to say.

Index

A

ABCDE model 39–40, 45, 167

ability, perceived lack of 37, 45

accountability 50, 62, 155–156

activities

  Circle of Control 99, 100

  clarity of language 212

  distraction log 145

  editing for your examiners 192

  growth mindset 35

  Human Function Curve 117

  prioritisation 104

  project team, identifying 50

  purpose, finding your sense of 15

  regulations, understanding 25

  routines

    shutdown 172

    startup 170

  signposting 204

  supervisory meeting agendas 73

  tasks for bad days 181

  time

    finding your most productive 109

    mapping 53

    scheduling 110–112

    using short blocks of 129

  writing

    audit 176

    fortress 132, 140

    prompts 159

Allen, David 127

ambiguity, reducing 194, 210

argument, emphasising 203

attention residue 141

B

backing up 56

bad days, dealing with 179–181

Bailey, Chris 145

BibTex (referencing tool) 138

boredom, combatting 157

Bradbury, Ray 131

brain 18, 135–137, 164–167

breaks 123, 180
   planning 61, 112, 113, 121
   in Pomodoro Technique 150,
      154
   from technology 146–149

C

caring responsibilities, and time
      management 60, 108,
      110

Carnegie, Dale 101

change, fear of 44

childcare, and time management
      60, 108, 110

Chimp Paradox 164–166

Circle of Concern 99, 100, 123

Circle of Control 99–100, 121

Circle of Influence 99, 100

Cirillo, Francesco 150

citations 88, 138
   checking 128, 181
   management tools 138, 139
   placeholders 139

Clear, James 169

coaching 32
   in supervisory relationship 70

coherence, of thesis 190, 198

comfort zone 115

Concern, Circle of 99, 100, 123

conclusions, mini 203

consistency
   in formatting of your thesis
      215, 218
   in language use 134, 192,
      194, 211
   of progress 163, 164
   in protecting your time 132
   in work scheduling 113, 120,
      122, 152

contingency planning 55–56

Control, Circle of 99–100, 121

Covey, Stephen R. 51, 99

critic, inner 38–39, 41, 45

cross-references 203

D

Darwin, Charles 101
   Darwin Days 179–181

deadlines
   extensions 54
   submission 25, 54
   in supervision 72

deep work 141–144, 161

depression 118, 119

details, editing of 194, 213–218, 219

diaries 174, 177

digital minimalism 146–149

distraction 145–148

and the Chimp Paradox 164–166

citations as 138

cost of 160

digital minimalism 146–149

fun versus annoying 145

identifying 145–148

internal/external 145, 146

internet rabbit holes 137–139, 146–149, 169

minimising 145–148

reference material 139

social media 142, 146–149, 173

spellcheckers 137

in workspace 140, 145, 146

distraction log 145, 161

distress 117, 118

downtime 112, 113, 121, 123, 148, 180

drafts, cycle of 134–135

Drama Triangle 74–77

E

editing 187, 193

argument, emphasising 203

for clarity 194, 205–209, 219

cross-references 203

cycle of 134–135

details 194, 213–218, 219

for your examiners 192

flow 194, 197–198, 219

headings, in thesis 203

mapping your thesis 194–197

mini-conclusions 203

outlines, chapter/section 202

paragraphs 198

proofreading 134, 194, 213–218

university regulations on 215

reverse outlining 198–201

scheduling 137

sentences 205–207

signposting 134, 194, 201–204, 219

stopping 221

structure 194, 194–197, 219

time needed for 218–220

versus writing 135–137, 162

Eisenhower Matrix 102–106, 121, 161

emotions

and feedback 86

fluctuating 31

freewriting about 167

frustration 157

and purpose, sense of 18

venting 166

EndNote (referencing tool) 138

examination process 21, 22,
    188–192

examiners 23, 188–192, 202

exercise, physical 105, 166

exhaustion 113, 114, 123, 180

extensions 54

F

fatigue 113, 114, 123, 136,
    180

feedback 83–87
  assessing 89
  disagreeing with 90
  format of 85
  implementing 86–87
  as opinion 89
  requesting 82, 85
  reviewing 87
  sources of 84
  from your supervisor 72, 85
  triaging 88
  troubleshooting problems 94
  types of 84

field, understanding of 190

flow, editing for 194, 197–198,
    219

Focusmate (website) 155

freewriting 158–159, 161, 162
  about emotions 167
  in shutdown routines 171
  in startup routines 169

frustration 157

G

goals, for sprints 58, 59

grammar 211

Grammarly (software) 217–218

growth mindset 34–35, 45

H

habits
  establishing 172–174
  triggers for 169–170, 173

handbooks, for PhD students
    23

headings, in thesis 203

health
  Human Function Curve 115–
    117, 121
  mental health 42, 105, 117,
    118–120
  prioritising 105, 113–114

Hersey-Blanchard Model of Situational Leadership 69

Human Function Curve 115–117, 121

I

Imposter Syndrome 36–37

incentives 166, 172

Incompetence Sandwich 33

independence, developing your 68–70

Influence, Circle of 99, 100

inner critic, defeating 38–39, 41, 45

Intention to Submit processes 81

internet rabbit holes 137–139, 146–149, 169

J

Johnston, Sue 188, 189, 202

journals/journalling 174, 177

K

Karpman, Stephen 74

Kiley, Margaret 18

L

Lamott, Anne 135

language use
  ambiguous 210
  consistency 134, 192, 194, 211
  grammar 211
  nominalisations 208
  power verbs 207
  related words 211
  sentences 205–207
  unnecessary words 211
  zombie nouns 208

Lennington, Michael 57

limits
  setting 22–23, 53, 179
  word 23

M

mapping
  your thesis 194–197
  your time 53

Mark, Gloria 160

Mendeley (referencing tool) 138

mental health 42, 105, 117, 118–120

milestones 57, 59, 66, 81

mind management models 34–35, 39–40, 45, 164–166, 167

mindset
  fixed 34, 36, 45

growth 34–35, 45

mini-conclusions 203

Moran, Brian P. 57

motivation 15–17
  and the Chimp Paradox 164–166
  cost of inaction 228
  during editing 220
  emotional 18
  loss of 27, 117
  recovering 115, 157, 180

Mullins, Gerry 18

multitasking 141, 142

N

narrative, interior 34

neuroscience 18, 135–137, 164–166

Newport, Cal 141–144, 147

Nixon, Peter 115

nominalisations 208

O

originality 19–20, 27, 36, 190

outlines, chapter/section 202

P

parenting responsibilities
  and planning 60

and time management 108, 110

Pareto Principle 179

Pareto, Vilfred 179

perfectionism, avoiding 178–179

persecutors, in the Drama Triangle 75, 76, 77, 78

Peters, Steve 164

PhD (Doctor of Philosophy)
  definition of 10, 18–20
  as examination 21
  practice-based 23
  progress of 31
  purpose of 14, 17
  quitting, consideration of 27
  requirements of 18–20
    originality 19–20, 27, 36, 190
    rigour 190
    significance 21, 27, 190
  stages of 51

planning 46–54, 157
  breaks 61
  contingency 55–56
  for deep work 142–145
  editing 218–220
  goals 58, 59
  milestones 57, 59, 66, 81
  and paid work 61

and parenting responsibilities 60

PhD as a project 47

problems, anticipating 55–56, 60

project team 48–50

review points 177–178

short-term 171

supervisors, discussion with 81–83

and writing audits 177

plans

sprints 56–59, 81, 177, 218

weekly 110–112, 126–127

Pomodoro Technique 149–151

positive psychology 39–40

power verbs 207

practice-based PhDs 23

present time, focusing on 32, 101

Pressfield, Stephen 156

prioritisation 97

Circle of Control 99–100, 121

of competing priorities 122, 129

Eisenhower Matrix 102–106, 121, 161

of your health 105, 113–114

saying no 106–107

and time management 102–106

problems, anticipating 55–56, 60

procrastination 104, 105

overcoming 156

productivity

and time management 109

writing 154, 178

progress

charts 166, 174

consistent 163, 164

evidence of 166, 171, 175

measuring 175–176

review points 177–178

project team 48, 105

project, treating your PhD as 47

prompts, writing 158, 161

proofreading 134, 194, 213–218

university regulations on 215

purpose

of the PhD 14, 17

your sense of 15–17, 18, 157

Q

quick wins 169

R

readers, of your thesis 22, 188–192

reference material 139

references 88
  checking 128
  management tools 138, 139
  placeholders 139
  verifying 181

regulations 23, 25, 181
  changing supervisors 79–80
  on extensions 54
  Intention to Submit process-es 81
  proofreading 215

rescuers, in the Drama Triangle 75, 76, 77, 78

RescueTime (software) 149

rest 112, 113, 121, 123, 148, 180

retreats 144

reverse outlining 198–201

review
  of feedback 87
  of progress 177–178
  of time management 112

rewards 166, 172

rigour 190

rituals 168

routines 167–169
  shutdown 171–172
  startup 168–169
  triggers for 169–170
  troubleshooting 183

S

scheduling
  editing 137
  planning 51
  time 108–112, 121
  work 113, 120, 122, 152
  writing 111, 121, 137

scope creep 24

scripts 167–169
  shutdown 171–172
  startup 168–169
  triggers for 169–170
  troubleshooting 183

Seligman, Martin 39

setbacks 33

shutdown routines 171–172

Shut up and Write sessions 155

significance 21, 27, 190

signposting 134, 194, 201–204, 219

Sinek, Simon 18

social media 142, 146–149, 173

sources, secondary, overreliance on 200

spellcheckers 137, 217–218

sprints 56–59, 81
  for editing 218
  goals 58, 59
  and writing audits 177

startup routines 168–169

stationery 104

strain zone 115, 117

stress 118

stretch zone 115, 117

structure
  editing 194, 194–197, 219
  and word count 24

submission 222
  deadlines 25, 54
  delays to 81, 82
  extensions 54
  Intention to Submit processes 81

supervisors
  changing 79–80, 95
  communication approaches 72, 85, 90, 95
  conflict, dealing with 74–77
  definition 10
  feedback from 72 ,85, 94
  meetings, agendas for 72, 73

multiple 74, 94
  and planning 47
  plans, discussion with 81–83
  in project team 48
  regulations, variable knowledge of 23
  relationships, managing 71–73, 95
  role, adapting 68–70
  and submission 222
  workloads of 76, 79

support, sources of 23, 118
  for mental health 119
  project team 48, 105
  in universities 27, 28, 56, 96

T

tasks
  for bad days 179–181
  dividing work into 151, 157
  short 128, 129
  switching 141, 142
  systematic 128

technology
  backing up 56
  citation management tools 139
  digital minimalism 146–149
  Focusmate (website) 155
  Grammarly (software) 217–218

RescueTime (software) 149

terminology 10, 11

thesis

  backing up 56

  definition of 10, 18–20

  'good enough' 22

  limits of 22–23

  mapping 194–197

  perfect, no such thing as 83

  purpose of 14, 17

  readers of 22, 188–192

  word limits 23

Thomson, Pat 204

tiaras, disappointing lack of 23

time

  available 127, 128

  commitments 52, 61

  lack of 54, 64

  valuing your own 108

time management

  and caring responsibilities 60, 108, 110

  context 127, 128

  Eisenhower Matrix 102–106, 121, 161

  energy levels 127, 128

  Pomodoro Technique 149–151

  and prioritisation 102–106, 127, 129

reviewing 112

scheduling 108–112, 121

short sessions 128, 129

for writing

  best time to write 108–109

  protecting 130–132

Trollope, Anthony 143

troubleshooting

  change, fear of 44

  deep work 161

  distractions 184

  editing 225

  exhaustion 123

  feedback problems 94

  fixed mindset 45

  focus, loss of 123, 185

  inner critic, defeating 45

  lack of ability, fear of 45

  motivation, lack of 27

  multiple supervisors 94

  originality, perceived lack of 27

  planning 65

  priorities, competing 122

  problems, anticipated 65

  procrastination 162

  routines 183

  significance, perceived lack of 27

  supervisory relationship 94–96

thesis requirements 28

time, lack of 64

writing versus editing 162

U

universities

regulations 23, 25

  changing supervisors 79–80

  on extensions 54

  Intention to Submit processes 81

  proofreading 215

  support for PhD students 27, 28, 56, 96

V

victims, in the Drama Triangle 75, 76, 77, 78

visualisation techniques, inner critic, defeating 38–39

viva 22

vocabulary

ambiguous 210

nominalisations 208

power verbs 207

related 211

unnecessary 211

zombie nouns 208

W

'why?' questions

and procrastination 156

and purpose, sense of 18

Win-Win outcomes 77

word choices

ambiguous 210

nominalisations 208

power verbs 207

related 211

unnecessary 211

zombie nouns 208

word count, tracking 176

word limit 23

work, paid 32, 61

and time management 109–110

worksheets

12-week sprint 59

30-Day Challenge 174

ABCDE model 41

Circle of Control 99

completion planner 53

distraction log 145

purpose of PhD 17

scheduling 110

supervisory meeting agendas 73

writing audit 175

workspace 130–132, 140, 181

distractions in 145, 146

in shutdown routines 172

in startup routines 169

writing

audits 175

best time for 108–109

cycle of 134–135

versus editing 135–137, 162

freewriting 158–159, 161,
        162

about emotions 167

in shutdown routines 171

in startup routines 169

journals/journalling 174, 177

language use

ambiguous 210

consistency 134, 192, 194,
        211

grammar 211

nominalisations 208

power verbs 207

related words 211

unnecessary words 211

zombie nouns 208

locations for 130–132, 140,
        145, 146, 169, 181

longhand 137

neuroscience and 135–137

productivity 154, 178

prompts 158, 161

scheduling 111, 121, 137

time, protecting 130–132

writing fortress 130–132, 140

Z

zombie nouns 208

Zotero (referencing tool) 138